Andreas A. Reil

Fachwörterbuch

Foto, Film & Fernsehen

deutsch - englisch / englisch - deutsch
sowie eine Übersicht der wichtigsten Abkürzungen

7. überarbeitete Auflage

D1691947

mediabook Verlag

7. Auflage
© Gau-Heppenheim 2002

mediabook Verlag

Dipl.- Ing. Andreas A. Reil
Grabenstraße 5
D - 55234 Gau-Heppenheim

Tel. +49 (67 31) 49 67 91
Fax +49 (67 31) 49 67 92
www.mediabook-verlag.de
info@mediabook-verlag.de

Inhaltsverzeichnis

deutsch - englisch —————————————— 7

englisch – deutsch —————————————— 111

Abkürzungen —————————————————— 221

Vorwort zur 7. Auflage

Das Fachwörterbuch Foto, Film & Fernsehen liegt nunmehr in der 6. Auflage vor, wieder in einigen Details verbessert und ergänzt. Seit der ersten Auflage 1988 hat es sich zum vielbenutzten Begleiter entwickelt.

Immer steht noch an erster Stelle die Übersichtlichkeit, die viele Benutzer von Standardwörterbüchern vermissen und die den Umgang mit diesen Büchern so kompliziert macht.

Wegen dieser Übersichtlichkeit wurde auch auf die Erklärung und Zuordnung der einzelnen Begriffe zu den jeweiligen Fachgebieten verzichtet. Hier ist der Fachmann gefragt, der sowohl über ein solides Grundwissen der englischen Sprache als auch ein ausgeprägtes Fachwissen verfügt. Auf dieser Basis wird er auch schnell herausfinden, welche der angebotenen Übersetzungen die richtige für das gesuchte Fachgebiet ist.

Gerne nehme ich Vorschläge für Ergänzungen und Verbesserungen entgegen, bei allen, die in die nächste Auflage übernommen werden, bedanke ich mich mit einem kostenlosen Exemplar. Nutzen Sie die elektronischen Medien und mailen Sie mir Ihre Vorschläge an fachbuch@web.de zu.

Gau-Heppenheim, im Juli 2002

deutsch - englisch

A

Abbau – deconstruction
Abbildungsebene – image plane
Abbildungsfehler – aberration defect, image defect
Abbildungsmaßstab – image scale
Abblende – fade out
abblenden (die Blende) – to set the stop, to stop down
abblenden (eine Szene) – to black out, to fade, to wipe off
Abdeckfolie – tissue
Abdeckung – matte, vignette; vor Lampen: cookie, cucaloris
abdrehen – to finish, to complete
Abdruck – copy
abdunkeln – to dim
abendfüllender Film – full length film
Abendkasse – box office
Abendlicht – sunset light
Abendprogramm – evening program
Abenteuerfilm – adventure film
Aberration – aberration
aberrationsfrei – aberration free
Abfalleimer – bin
abgebrochene Aufnahme – false start
abgedrehter Film – the film is in the can
abgedroschen – hackneyed
abgekaschtes Bild – truncated picture
abgelenkter Strahl – deflected beam
abgeschirmtes Kabel – shielded cable
Abgleich – adjustment, alignment, set up
abgleichen – to align, to set up
Abhandlung – treatment
abhören – to listen
Abhörpegel – reproducing level
Abhörraum – monitor room
Abhörtisch – sound monitoring apparatus
abisolieren – to bare the wires
abklammern – to clip
A/B Kopierverfahren – A and B printing

Ablagerung – incrustation
Ablaufplan – running order
Ablaufregisseur – continuity director
Ablenkeinheit – deflector, scanning component
Ablenkfehler – deflection distortion, pattern distortion
Ablenkplatte – deflecting electrodes, deflector plate
Ablenkung – deflection
Ablesefehler – reading error
Abnahmekopie – final trial composite
abnehmen – to decrease
Abonnentenfernsehen – pay-TV
abschalten – eighty six (*slang*), to kill
Abschirmkappe – screening can
Abschluß des Fernsehkabels – matching of a television aerial, matching of an antenna cable
Abschlußwiderstand – terminal resistance
Abschminktuch – tissue
Abschwächer – reducer
Abschwächung einer Kopie – lightening of a print
absorbieren – to absorb
Absorptionsfilter – absorption filter
Abspann – end titles
Abspielfehler – playback loss, reproducing loss
Abstand der Perforationslöcher – spacing of perforation holes, perforation gauge
abstauben – to dust
abstimmen – to tune
Abstimmgerät – tuning variometer
Abstimmung – tuning
Abtasteinheit – scanning device
abtasten – to scan
abtastender Elektronenstrahl – scanning beam
Abtaster – scanner
Abtastgeschwindigkeit – pick-up velocity
Abtastscheibe – hunting disk
Abtastspalt – scanning gap
Abtaststrahl – scanning beam
Abtastung – scanning
Abtastvorrichtung – sweep device

Abteilungsleiter – head of department
abtropfen – to drain
Abweichung – aberration, variation
Abweichung zwischen Sucherbild und dem Bildfenster – view-finder mismatch
Abwickelkassette – feed magazine
Abwickelrolle, Abwickelspule – delivery spool, feed reel, film feeding, supply reel, supply spool, take-up reel
Abwickelseite – feed side
Abzug – copy, print
Acetatfilm – acetate film
Achromat, achromatisches Objektiv – achromatic lens, achromate
achromatisch – achromatic, achromatically
Achromatismus – achromatism
Achssprung – crossing the line, frame jumps
Achtung! Aufnahme! – »Stand by!«
»Achtung, Aufnahme!«, Anweisung an den Kameramann – »Action! Start grinding!«, »Camera! Action!« bei MAZ: »Start Rolling!«
Adapter – adapter
additives Farbverfahren – additive color process
Agentur – agency
eine Agenturmeldung absetzen – to put out
AK – dailies (US), rush (GB), picture daily print, rushes (GB), rush print (GB), working print, work print
Akku – battery, power pack
Akkugürtel – battery belt
Akkulicht – battery lighting
Akkumulatorzelle – cell of an accumulator
Aktmodell – life model, nude
Akustik – acoustics
akustische Raumgestaltung – room acoustics
akustischer Kurzschluß – acoustical short circuit
akustischer Scheinwiderstand – acoustic impedance, acoustical resistance
akustische Rückkopplung – acoustical back coupling, acoustical feedback, howl round
akustischer Wirkungsgrad – acoustical efficiency
akustische Schwingung – acoustical oscillation
akzeptierte Aufnahme – »Wrap!«, »It's a wrap!«
Alkalizelle – alkaline battery, alkaline metal-cell

allgemeines Gemurmel in einer Massenszene – walla-walla
Allonge – identification leader, leader
als Partner des Hauptdarstellers spielen – to act opposite the star
alternierender Burst – alternating burst, swinging burst
Alterung – aging
Altist – alto, alto-singer
Altstimme – alto, alto voice
Aluminiumkamerakoffer – aluminum camera case
Ambiente – ambience
amerikanische Einstellung – two-shot
amerikanische Nacht – day-for-night, night effect
Ampère – intensity of current
Ampèremeter – ammeter
Ampèrestunde – ampere-hour
Amplitudenbegrenzer – amplitude separation circuit, amplitude separation lopper, peak limiter
Amplitudenmodulation – amplitude modulation
Amplitudenschwankungen – amplitude variations
Ampltitudenaufschaukelung – amplitude increase
Anachromat, anachromatisches Objektiv – anachromatic lens
Anaglyph – anaglyphe
Anaglyphenbrille – anaglyphe spectacles
Anaglyphenverfahren – anaglyphe process
Anamorphose – anamorphose
Anamorphot – anamorphotic lens
anamorphotische Einrichtung – anamorphotic attachment
anamorphotischer Spiegel – anamorphotic mirror
anamorphotisches Objektiv – anamorphotic lens, squeete lens
anamorphotisches System – anamorphotic system
anamorphotische Zylinderlinse – cylindrical anamorphoser
anamorphotisch gepreßtes Negativ – anamorphotic squeezed negative
Anastigmat – anastigmat
anastigmatisches Objektiv – anastigmatic lens
Anastigmatismus – anastigmatism
Andruckfenster – pressure gate
Andruckglasscheibe – platen
Andruckkufe (am Bildfenster) – pressure pad (on the gate)
Andruckplatte – pressure plate
Andruckrolle – pressing roller

Anfänger – beginner, newcomer
Anfangseinstellung, gibt einen Überblick über die Szene – establishing shot
Anfertigen eines Nachrichtenfilms – news material preparation, preparation of news material
angeregter Leuchtstoff – exited phosphor
angeschlossener Sender – joint transmitter
Anhebung – emphasis
Anhebungsfilter – accentuation filter
Anodenspannung – plate voltage
Anpaßring – step-up ring
Ansager – narrator, announcer, video announcer
Anschluß – connector
Anschlußkabel – connection cable
Anschlußszene – connecting scene
Anschnitt – cut-in scene
ansetzen – to mix
Ansprechzeit für Limiter – attack time
Ansteckmikrofon, Anstecker – lapel microphone, personal microphone
Antenne – antenna
Antennenabstimmung – antenna matching
Antennenanschluß – antenna pick-up
Antennenausgang – aerial output, antenna output
Antenneneingang – aerial input, antenna input
Antennenelement – aerial element, antenna element
Antennenmast – antenna mast, radio mast
Antennenrotor – antenna rotor
Antennensignal – aerial signal, antenna signal
Antennenverstärker – multi-coupler, distributing amplifier
Antennenweiche – antenna diplexer, antenna two-way splitter
Antennenwirkfläche – effective area of antenna
Antireflexbelag einer Linse – antireflex layer of a lens
Antischleiermittel – anti-fog agent
Antriebsmotor – drive motor
Anwendungsbereich – range of adaptilities
Anzahl der Linsen – number of elements
Anzeige – display
Anzeige, Inserat – advertisement, publicity
Anzeigeinstrument – display, indicator, meter

Apertur – aperture
Aperturblendenfehler – aperture diaphragm error
Aperturkorrektur – aperture correction (GB), aperture compensating (GB), aperture equalization (US)
Aplanat – aplanat
Apochromat – apochromat
Arbeitsbedingungen – working conditions
Arbeitsflügel einer Umlaufblende – working wing of a rotating shutter
Arbeitskopie – working print, work print
Arbeitslicht – work light
Arbeitslösung – working solution
Arbeitsphase – processing step
Arbeitsrichtlinien – working instructions
Arbeitsspannung – working voltage, working volt
Arbeitstitel – provisional title, working title
Architekturaufnahme – architectural view
Archiv – film archive, library of stock shots
Archivaufnahme – stock shot
Archivhülle – file
archivieren – to put in the library
Archivnegativ – negative for archives purposes
Arrangeur – aranger
Astigmatismus – astigmatism
asymetrischer Anastigmat – asymmetrical anastigmat
asynchron – non-sync, non-synchron, out of sync
asynchrone Tonaufnahme – wild recording
Asynchronmotor – asynchronous motor
Atelier – floor, set, shooting studio, studio
Atelierarbeiter – stage hand
Atelierarbeiter, für den Dolly, Kamerafahrten und Kameraumbau zuständig – grip
Atelieraufnahme – studio shot
Atelierleitung – studio management
Ateliersekretärin – continuity girl
Atmo – room noise, room sound, room tone, wild sound
audiovisuelle Unterrichtsmittel – audiovisual aids
auf Abruf – on call
Aufbau einer Außenszene im Studio – studio exteriors
Aufbewahrung – storage

Aufbewahrungskasten – storage box
Aufblende – dissolve-in, fade-in
aufblenden – to fade-in, to wipe-on
Aufhängvorrichtung für Lampen von der Beleuchterbrücke – bazooka
Aufheizzeit – warming-up time, warm-up time
Aufheller, Aufhellicht – booster light, fill-in light, fill light, filler, kicker light
Aufhellschirm, Aufhellwand – brighting screen
Aufhellung (außen) – booster light
Aufhellung einer Kopie – lightening of a print
Auflage – run
Auflagegewicht – stylus force, tracking force
Auflagemaß – tracking, back focus
Auflicht – bias light
Auflichtdensitometer – reflection densitometer
Auflösung – definition, picture definition, resolution
Auflösungsvermögen – resolving power
aufmöbeln – to pep up
Aufnahme – shot, take
Aufnahmeatelier – shooting studio
Aufnahme aus dem Auto – rolling shot
Aufnahme aus großer Entfernung – long shot
Aufnahme aus kurzer Entfernung – short-distance shot
Aufnahmebedingung – recording conditions
Aufnahmebereitschaft – stand-by
Aufnahmebericht – dope sheet, continuity report
Aufnahmebildwinkel – shooting angle
Aufnahme durch eine Maske – matte shot
Aufnahmeeinheit – equipment, outfit, pick-up equipment
Aufnahmeentfernung – shooting distance, shooting field
Aufnahmefrequenzgang – frequency response of recording
Aufnahmegeschwindigkeit – speed of taking
Aufnahmegeschwindigkeit für Ton – sound record speeding
Aufnahme im Halbdunkel – twilight shot
Aufnahmekanal – production recording channel
Aufnahmeleiter – floor manager, first assistant, unit manager, location manager
Aufnahme mit drei Darstellern – three-shot
Aufnahme mit einem Darstellern – single, single shot

Aufnahme mit zwei Darstellern – two-shot
Aufnahmeobjektiv – taking lens
Aufnahme ohne Kamerabewegung – static shot
Aufnahmeplan – film schedule, shooting pattern, shooting plan, shooting schedule
Aufnahmerekorder – master recorder
Aufnahmerichtung der Kamera – camera direction
Aufnahmeröhre – pick-up tube
Aufnahmerückschau – review
Aufnahmestab – staff
Aufnahmestudio – floor
Aufnahmesystem – recording system
Aufnahmeteam – crew, team, unit
Aufnahmeverfahren – filming technique
Aufnahmeverstärker – recording amplifier
Aufnahme-Wiedergabekopf – combined recording-reproducing head
Aufnahme-Wiedergabeverstärke – record-reproduce amplifier
eine Aufnahme wiederholen – re-take, reticulation
Aufnahmewinkel – acceptance angle, shooting angle
aufrechtstehendes Bild – upright image
Aufsager in die Kamera – camera talk, stand-up
Aufsichtsgraukeil – gray card
Aufsprechstrom – recording current
aufstellen – to rig
aufteilen – to subdivide
Aufwickelseite – take-up side
Aufwickelspule – take-up reel
Aufzeichungsgeschwindigkeit – writing speed
aufziehen (Bilder) – to mount
aufziehen, die Brennweite verkürzen – zoom-away shot, zoom-out shot
Augenlicht – basher, camera light, camera headlamp, eyelight
Augenträgheit – persistence of vision
ausbleichen – to bleach out
Ausblendschalter – Fader
aus dem Bildausschnitt aussparen – to crop
ausdrucksloser Schauspieler – actor without expression
auseinanderschraubare Filmspule – split reel, split spool
Ausfallswinkel – angle of deflection
Ausgang – output

Ausgangsspannung – output level
ausgefressenes Negativ – snoot and white wash (*slang*)
ausgefressen, überbelichteter Film – bleached out
Ausgleich der Geschwindigkeitsdifferenz zwischen Film und Fernsehbildern – picture join
Ausgleichsentwickler – compensating developer
Auslandskorrespondent – foreign correspondent
Auslöser – release, trigger
Ausmustern – daily assembling
Ausrüstung – equipment, outfit
Ausrüstung für Luftbildaufnahmen – aerial equipment
Ausrüstung für Unterwasseraufnahmen – sub-aqua equipment
Ausschließlichkeitsrechte – exclusive rights
Ausschnitt – opening, cut, cut out
»Aus«, »Schnitt!« (Ende einer Szene), Anweisung des Regisseurs an den Kameramann – »Cut!«
Außenarbeit – outdoor location work
Außenaufnahme – exterior shot, location shot, on location
Außendurchmesser des Objektivanschlußes – outside diameter of lens mount
Außenproduktion, Außenreportage – field production
Außenproduktion mit Fernsehkameras – electronic field production
Außenübertragung – field pickup, nemo, OB, outside broadcast, remote production
außerhalb des Blickwinkels der Kamera – out of frame
Aussetzfehler – drop-out
ausspiegeln – to reflect out
ausspülen – to rinse
Ausstatter – set decorator
Ausstatter für spezielle Requisiten – prop maker
Ausstattung (im Vor-oder Nachspann) – set decoration (in the title of a film)
Ausstattungsfilm – spectacle picture
Ausstellung – exhibition (GB), exposition (US)
Aussteuerungsanzeige – volume indicator
Ausstrahlung eines Films – running, televising of a film
austasten – to blank
Austastschulter – front porch, back porch
Austastsignal – black-out signal, blanking signal

Austastung – black-out (US), blanking (GB)
Austastung des Bildsignals – black-out of the video signal (US), blanking of the video signal (GB)
Austrittswinkel – angle of emergence
ausverkauftes Kino – sold-out theatre
auswählen – to select
auswechselbarer Balgen – interchangeable bellows
auswechselbares Bildfenster – convertible film gate
auswechselbares Suchersystem – interchangeable finder system
Auswertung eines Films – exploitation of a film
Auswertungsrechte – distribution rights
ausziehbares Bodenstativ, ausziehbares Lampenstativ – telescopic floor stand
Autokino – drive-in cinema
automatische Blendensteuerung – automatic aperture control, auto iris
automatische Fokussierung – autofocus
automatische Lautstärkeregelung – automatic volume control
automatische Phasenregelung – automatic phase control
automatische Springblende – automatic diaphragm
Autor – writer
Autorenfilm – writer's own film
Autor komischer Filmszenen – gag-writer
Autostativ – automobile base, car mount, side car mount

B

Babystativ – baby legs
Bajonettfassung – bayonet mount
Bajonettverschluß – bayonet closing, bayonet joint
Balgen – bellows
Balgenauszug – bellow extension of camera
Balgenkompendium – bellows matte box
Ballettfilm – ballet feature
Band – tape
Bandabrieb – head wear
Bandandruck – contact pressure, head-to-tape pressure
Bandantriebsachse – capstan
Bandaufnahme – tape record
Bandbreite – band width
Banddehnung – band expansion, band spread, tape curvature
Bandführung – tape guide
Bandgerät – tape recorder
Bandgeschwindigkeit – tape speed
Bandlängenanzeiger – tape length indicator
Bandlauf – tape run
Bandlaufanzeige – tape run indicator
Bandmaterial für den 1-Zoll B-Standard (C-Standard) – video tape Type B (video tape Type C)
Bandrauschen – tape hiss, tape noise
Bandriß – tape break
Bandschleife – tape loop
Bandschlupf – tape slippage
Bandspieler – dubber
Bandstärke – thickness of tape
Bandstellenanzeiger – tape position indicator
Bandtransportrolle – capstan
Bandvorspann – leader of the tape
Bandzug – tape tension
Bandzugregelung – skew
BAS-Signal – video signal
Baßlautsprecher – woofer

Baßton – low sound
Batterie – battery
Batteriekontrolle – battery check
Bauteil – component
beabsichtiger Ton-Bild-Versatz – sound track advance, sound advance, sync advance
Bearbeiter – adaptator
Bearbeitung – adaption
Bedienungsanleitung – operating instructions
Bedienungsanweisung – instruction book, owners manual
Bedienungsvorschrift – working instructions
Begrenzer – limiter
Beiprogramm – additional film, fill-up film
Beleuchter – electrician, light electrician
Beleuchterbrücke – catwalk, gallery, gantry, light platform, rigging, scaffolding
Beleuchter, der die Lampen einschaltet – juicer (*slang*)
Beleuchtung – lighting
die Beleuchtung ausschalten – to save the lights
Beleuchtung mit 3 Lampen – triangle lighting
Beleuchtung mit einer im Bild sichtbaren Deckenlamp – pool-hall lighting
Beleuchtungsstärke – illumination level
Beleuchtungstechnik mit großem Kontrastumfang – low key
Beleuchtungstechnik mit kleinem Kontrastumfang – high key
belichteter Film, der durch die Kamera lief – camera master
Belichtung – exposure
Belichtungsmesser – exposure meter, light meter, photometer
Belichtungsprobe – exposure test
Belichtungsspielraum – exposure tolerance, latitude
Belichtungssteuerung – exposure control
Belichtungszeit – exposure time, speed, speed rating
Bereitschaftstasche – camera case
Beruhigungsflügel eines Umlaufverschlusses – anti-flicker blade of a rotating shutter, anti-flicker vane of a rotating shutter
beschichtetes Objektiv – coated lens
Beschneiden der tiefen und hohen Frequenzen mit Filtern – roll-off
Beschreibung – scanning

Besetzung – cast, characters
bester Visus – 20/20, best view
bestimmen des Bildausschnitts – framing
Bestimmung des Kopierlichts – timing of printing light
Betonung – emphasis
Betrachtungswinkel – viewing angle
Betriebsartenumschalter – change-over switch
betriebsbereit – in working order
Betriebsspannung – working voltage, working volt
Betriebsunfall – accident in working
Beugung – diffraction
Bewegung – agitation
Bezugsband – reference tape
Bezugspegel für Schwarz – black reference level
Biaslicht – light bias
biegsame Welle – flexible shaft
bikonkav – double concave
Bild – frame, image, picture
Bildablenkgenerator – framing oscillator
Bildablenkung – picture scan
Bildabtastung – picture scanning
Bildarchiv – photo library, stills library
Bildaufnahmebericht – camera sheet, dope sheet
Bildaufnahmegeschwindigkeit – speed of taking
Bildaufnahmeröhre – pick-up tube, television tube, tube
Bild aus der Unschärfe in die Schärfe ziehen – to refocus, to focus up
Bildausfall – vision break
Bildausschnitt – framing
Bildausschnitt festlegen – to frame
Bildaussteuerung – picture control
Bildbetrachter – film viewer
Bildbreitenregler – horizontal size control
Bild, das aus zwei Teilbildern im Zeilensprungverfahren gebildet wird, Vollbild des Fernsehens – two-field picture, frame
Bilddiagonale – image diagonal
Bilddurchlauf – picture slip
Bildebene – image point
Bildeinstellvorrichtung – framing carriage

Bildendverstärker – image power amplifier
Bilder aufziehen – to laminate, to mount
Bilder pro Sekunde – frames per second
Bildexpansion – line pulling
Bildfang – holding control
Bildfangregler – framing control, vertical hold control
Bildfehler – picture geometry fault
Bildfeld – camera coverage, area of the picture
Bildfeldwölbung – curvature of image field, curvature of field
Bildfenster – aperture, film gate, picture gate, picture window
Bildfenster für Breitwandformat – wide screen aperture film gate
Bildfenster für Normalfilmformat – academy format film gate
Bildfenster für Stummfilmformat – full aperture film gate
Bildflimmern – image flickering
Bildfolgefrequenz – picture repetition frequency
Bildformat – aspect ratio, picture ratio, covered image format, picture size
Bildgamma – picture gamma
Bildgeschwindigkeit – frames per second
Bildgleichlaufimpuls – picture sync pulse
Bildhelligkeit – video intensity
Bildhöhe – height of picture
Bild in die Unschärfe ziehen – to defocus
Bildinformation – picture information
Bildingenieur – shader, video engineer, vision control supervisor
Bildkanal – video channel
Bildkontrollgerät – picture and waveform monitor, wave form monitor
Bildkreisdurchmesser – angle of coverage, circle of illumination
Bildmaske – framing mask
Bildmischer – switcher
Bildmischpult – video mixing desk
Bildmitte – center of picture
Bildmuster – dailies (US), rush (GB), picture daily print, rushes, rush print (GB), working print, work print
Bild ohne Synchronton – wild picture
Bildplatte – videodisc
Bildpumpen – bouncing (US), jumping, vertical hunting (GB)
Bildpunkt – picture element, picture point, pixel

Bildpunkthelligkeit – brightness of the image spot, brilliance of the image spot
Bildqualität – picture quality
Bildrauschen – picture noise
Bildregieraum – apparatus room, camera control room, video control room, vision control room
Bildröhre – pick-up tube, tube, viewing screen
Bildschärfe – definition of the picture
Bildschirm – viewing screen
Bildschnitt – picture editing
Bildschramme – scratch
Bildschritt – frame gauge
Bild-Seitenverhältnis – aspect ratio, picture ratio
Bildsignal – picture signal
Bildspeicherplatte – image retaining panel
Bildspeicherröhre – image storing tube
Bildsprung – jump cut
Bildspur – video track
Bildstabilisator – image stabilizer
Bildstand – picture steadyness, steadyness of image
Bildsteg – rack line
Bildstörung – image interference
Bildstrich – frame-line
Bildstricheinstellung – framing
den Bildstrich nach oben verstellen – to frame up
den Bildstrich nach unten verstellen – to frame down
Bildtechniker – switcher, technical director, vision mixer
Bild-Ton Abstand – distance between sound and image
Bild-Tonträger Abstand – vision to sound-carrier spacing
Bildträger – picture carrier, vision carrier
Bildträgerabstand – adjacent picture carrier spacing
Bildüberblendung – picture change-over
Bildübertragung – image transmission
Bildumschalter – video switch
Bild- und Tonschaltraum – central apparatus room
Bildverzerrung – anamorphose
Bildwandabdeckung – screen mask
Bildwandler – image sensor

Bildwandlerröhre – image converter tube
Bildwechselzahl – image frequency
Bildweite – image distance
Bildwinkel – angle of view, angular field, lens angle, picture angle
Bildzahl – number of frames
Bildzähler – exposure counter, frame counter
Bildzittern – jitter
»Bitte das Bild frei machen!« – »Please clear (the) camera!«
Blankfilm – clear leader
blankieren – to polish
Blankierung – lacquering
Blankschramme – celluloid scratch
Blankseite – side of celluloid
blauempfindlich – blue sensitive
Blaufilter – blue filter
blaugrün. – cyan
Blaupause – blue-print
Blaustich – blue overcast
blaustichig – bluish tinged
Bleichbad – bleach
Bleichfixierbad – bleach fix, bleach fixing bath
Blende – aperture stop, diaphragm, stop
Blende (optische) – fade
die Blende einstellen – to set the stop
Blende, Lichtblende – flag
blenden – to wipe
Blendenöffnung – aperture
Blendenring – diaphragm ring
Blendenzahl – stop
Blickrichtung von Schauspielern – eye line
Blickwinkel eines Aufnahmeobjektivs – field of view
blinder Fleck (Auge) – fovea
blitzen, Blitzlichtaufnahme machen – to take photoflash picture
Blitzlichtaufnahme – flash light photography
Blitzlicht, Blitzlichtgerät – flashgun, flash
Blitzschuh – flash-shoe
Blitzsynchronisation – flash synchronization
Blitzwürfel – flash cube

Blue-Screen Verfahren – blue box process, blue screen process
Bobby – core
Bobby mit 75mm (50mm) Durchmesser – Z core (T core)
Bodenhöhe – floor level, ground level
Bodenstativ – telescopic floor stand
Bogenkamerafahrt – arcing
Bogenlampe – arc lamp
Braunsche Röhre – Braun tube, cathode-ray tube
braunschwarzer Toner – brown-black tone
Breitbandverstärker – wide-range amplifier
Breitwand – wide-screen
Breitwandfilm – wide-screen film
Breitwandverfahren – wide-screen system
Brennebene – focal plane
Brenner – bulb
Brennpunkt – focal point
Brennweite – focal length
die Brennweite verkürzen, aufziehen – zoom-away shot, zoom-out shot
die Brennweite verlängern, verdichten – zoom-in shot
Brennweitenbereich – zoom range, zoom ratio
Brennweitenverdoppler – extender, range ~, tele-converter
Brillanz – brilliancy
Broschüre – prospectus
Bromsilberpapier – bromide paper
brummfrei – hum-free
Brummspannung – a.c. ripple voltage, hum voltage
brünieren – to brown
Brustbild – head-and-shoulder portrait
Bruststütze – breast-tripod
Buch – scenario, script, shooting script
Buchse – female plug
Bühne – floor, set, shooting studio, studio
Bühnenarbeiter – floor man, set dresser
Bühnenarbeiter, für Dolly, Kran und Kameraumbauten zuständig – grip
Bühnenbild – scenery
Bühnenbildner – art director
Bühnengewicht – sandbag, stage weight
Bühnenkiste – apple box, pancake

Bühnenlicht – work light
Bühnen-oder Dekorationsvordergrund – downstage
Bühnenvorhang – stage curtain
Burst – burst, color burst
B-Y Matrix – B-Y matrix, blue-color matrix difference
B-Y Signal – B-Y signal, blue color difference signal

C

Calliereffekt, Callierfaktor – Callier's effect, Callier's quotient
Carnet – carnet, tempex
C-Fassung – C-mount
Chamois – cream
Charakterdarsteller – character actor
Chargennummer – batch number, emulsion number
Chefdramaturg – scenario editor
Choreograf – dance director
chromatische Aberration – chromatical aberration
Chromgelb – chrome yellow
Chrominanzsignal – chrominance signal
Chrominanzträgerversetzung – subcarrier offset
C-Klemme – C-clamp
C-MOS Chip – photo-conducting camera tube
C-Mount Adapter – C-mount adapter
Commag (*Codewort*) – combined print, married stripe (GB), synchronized print, comopt (*Codewort*)
Comopt (*Codewort*) – composite print, married print (GB), syn commag (*Codewort*)
Compurverschluß – compur shutter
Computerbildspeicher – framebuffer
Cordband – magnetic film, perforated magnetic film
Co-Regisseur – associate director
Cover – cover, title page
Curriculum Vitae – curriculum vitae (US), resumé (GB)
Cutterassistent (in) – editor's assistant
Cutter, Cutterin – cutter, editor, film editor
Cyanblau – cyan

D

Dachkantprisma – roof prism
Dämmerung – dawn, magic hour
Darsteller – actor, interpret
Darstellerin – actress
mit einem Darsteller eine Rolle einstudieren – to coach an actor in a part
einen Darsteller hervorstellen – to favor
das Band wechseln – to change the tape
Dateneinbelichtung – date recording system
Deckgläschen – cover-glass
Dekoder – decoder
Dekoration – floor, scenery, set, shooting studio, studio
Dekorationsmaterial – props
Dekorationsvordergrund – downstage
Dekoration abbauen – to kill a set, to strike a set
Delta-L Korrektur – Delta-L correction, Delta-L system
Densitometrie – densitometry
deutsche Fassung eines Films – German version of a movie
Dialog – dialogue
Dialogautor – direction writer
Dialogregie – direction of dialogue
Dialogregisseur – dialog director
Diamagazin – slide tray
Diapositiv – slide, transparency
Diaprojektor – slide projector
Diarahmen – slide carrier, slide mount
Dias rahmen – to mount
Dichte – density
Differenzträger – inter carrier
Differenzträgerverfahren – carrier difference system
diffuse Vorbelichtung – preflash, prefof
Digitalanzeige – digital display
Diplom – award
direkte Beleuchtung – direct lighting
direkte Satellitenübertragung – direct broadcast by satellite
Dirigent – conductor

Diskussionsrunde – panel
Disponent (in) – booker
Dokumentarfilm – documentary
Dokumentarfilmkameramann – documentary cameraman
Dolly – camera dolly, dolly, truck
Dollyfahrer – dolly grip, tracker, travelling man
Doppelanastigmat – double anastigmat
Doppelbelichtung – double-exposure, superimposition
Doppelbelichtungssperre – double-exposure (prevention) lock
Doppelbild – double image, echo, fold-over, ghost picture (GB), multipath effect (US)
Doppelgänger – typecast
Doppelgängerbesetzung – dual role cast
Doppelkondensor – double condenser
Doppelkonus – double conus
doppelseitiger Sperrgreifer – double register pin
doppelseitig klebendes Klebeband – double-face tape
Doppelsperrgreifer – dual registration pin
Doppelvorstellung – double feature
Double (eines Darstellers) – stand-in, understudy
Drahtauslöser – cable release, shutter release, wire release
Drahtgaze – wire net scrim
drahtloses Mikrofon – radio microphone, wireless microphone
Dramaturg – story writer
Drehbeginn – to go into production, start of shooting
Drehbericht – log-sheet, report sheet
Drehbewegung – rotary action
Drehbuch – continuity, scenario, screenplay, (shooting)script
Drehbuchautor – scenarist, screenwriter
Drehbuchentwurf – treatment of the script, rough treatment
Drehbuch mit Details für jede Einstellung – film shooting script
Drehbühne – rotating floor
drehen – to crank, to film
Drehkondensator – rotary condenser, variable condenser
Drehort – locale, locality, scene of shooting
»Drehort nicht betreten!« Hinweisschild vor Studios – »Closed set!«
Drehpause – set brake, shooting break
Drehplan – film schedule, shooting pattern, shooting plan, shooting schedule

Drehspulinstrument – moving coil meter
Drehstrom – 3-phase current
Drehtag – shooting day
Drehteller – turntable
Drehverhältnis – cutting ratio, shooting ratio
Dreibeinstativ – 3-legged stand
3-D Film, dreidimensionaler Film – 3-D film
3-Röhrenkamera – 3-tube camera
30-Sekunden Fernsehspot – thirty
3-strahl Fernsehröhre – 3-gun picture tube
3-Strahlröhre – tricolor tube
3. Korrekturkopie – third answer print
dunkel – dark
Dunkelkammer – dark room, photographic dark room
Dunkelkammerbeleuchtung – safelight
Dunkelkammerlampe – laboratory lamp
Dunkelsack – changing bag
dunkler oder dumpfer Ton – all bottom sound
Dunstfilter – hazefilter
Duplikatnegativ – duplicating negative
Dup-Negativ – dup negative
Dup-Positiv – duplicate positive
durchbrennen – to burn out
Durchfahrgenehmigung – drive on permission
Durchfahrschein – gate pass
durchgehende Arbeitszeit – non-stop working time
durchgezeichnetes Negativ – negative with fine definition
Durchlaufbildkopiermaschine – continuous filmprinter
Durchlaufkopiermaschine für Bild und Ton – double-head continuous contact printer
Durchlaufprobe – run-through
Durchprojektion – back projection
durchschleifen eines Videosignals – video looping
durchschnittliche Bildhelligkeit – average picture level
Durchsichtsucher – brilliant finder, brilliant view-finder
Durchzeichnung bis in die Schatten – shadow detail
Dynamik, Dynamikbereich – S/N ratio

E

EB-Schneideraum – edit suite (GB)
EB-Techniker – tape man
Echobild – multi path effect (US)
Effektbeleuchtung – effect lighting
Effektscheinwerfer – effect spot
Eichgenerator – calibrator
Eichung – calibration
Eigenrauschen von Mikrofonen – microphone noise
einadriges Kabel – single-wire cable
einäugige Spiegelreflexkamera – single-lens-reflex camera
Einbandverfahren – single system
Einbeinstativ – monopod
einblenden – to dub in
Einblendmaterial – film footage
einbrennen – to burn in
Einbrennstelle in der Aufnahmeröhre – burn-in
Einergang – one-to-one action, single-picture action, stop motion
Einfallswinkel – angle of incidence
einfärben – to tint
Eingang – input
eingeführt. Eine Person oder ein Drehort, der bereits gezeigt wurde; auch: Personen, die in »Spago's« Restaurant, Hollywood, bekannt sind (*slang*) – established
eingelagertes Negativ – negative for archives purposes
eingestanzter Hintergrund – chroma-key backing
Einheitsmagazin – standard magazine
1kW Scheinwerfer – ashan
1kW Strahler – can
1kW Stufenlinsenscheinwerfer – ace
einkitten – to cement
einkopieren – to print in, to superimpose
einkopierter Titel – superimposed title
Einkopierung – composite shot
Einleuchten – setting of the lamps
Einlichtkopie – one-light print

einlicht Schwarzweißmuster – dirty dupe
Einmessen der Köpfe – to align the heads, heads alignment
Einnahmen – revenues
einpegeln – to line up
Einrichten der Einstellung – to frame
»Einsatz verpaßt!« – »Missed the cue!«
einschalten – to connect
einschleifen – to connect
einseitig perforiertes Filmmaterial – single perforation
einspielen – to earn
einstellbare Gewichtsausgleichfeder – adjustable counter balance spring
Einstellbild – flash frame
Einstellfilm – calibration reel
Einstellung, bei der die Kamera hinter die Kulissen der Dekoration sieht – shoot-off
eine Einstellung drehen – to shoot
eine Einstellung einrichten – to frame
Einstellung, die eine ganze Person zeigt – full shot
Einstellung mit drei Darstellern – three-shot
Einstellung mit einem Darstellern – single, single shot
Einstellung mit zwei Darstellern – two-shot
Einstellung von oben – overhead shot
Einstellwinkel – setting angle
Einstufenbildmischer – A-B cut mixer
Eintrittskarte – ticket
Eintrittspreis – admission fee
Eintritt verboten – keep off
Einzackenschrift bei Lichtton – single edge variable width track
Einzelbildaufnahme – successive frame exposure
Einzelbildauslöser – single-frame release
Einzelbildkamera – animation camera
Einzelbildmotor – stop motion motor
einzelnes Filmbild – film frame, frame
Eiweißlasur – albumen lazur
Elektretmikrofon – electret microphone
Elektriker – electrician, spark (*slang*), wiremann
elektrische Fernbedienung – remote cable switch
elektrische Spannung – electric tension (voltage)

Elektroakustik – electro acoustics
elektromagnetisches Spektrum – electromagnetic spectrum
Elektronenkanone – electron gun
elektronischer Abgleich – adjustment, alignment, set up
elektronischer Bildverbesserer – enhancer
elektronischer Kameraabgleich – camera set-up
elektronischer Schnitt – electronic editing, electronic cut
Empfänger – reciever
Empfangsbereich – coverage, service area, range of reception
Empfangsgrenzgebiet – fringe area
Empfang über Antenne – antenna reception
Empfang über Kabel – cable reception
empfindlich – sensitive
Empfindlichkeit – speed
Empfindlichkeit einer Aufnahmeröhre – radiant sensitivity of a camera tube
Emulsion – emulsion
Emulsionsnummer – emulsion number
Endband – tail leader
Ende eines Drehtags – wrap
Endfassung – final draft
Endkopie – final trial composite
Endmischband – final composite track, master sound track
Endmischung – final mix
Endverstärker – booster amplifier, main amplifier, power amplifier
engagieren – to cast
Ensemble – cast, crew
entfernen – to remove
Entfernungsbereich – focusing range
Entfernungseinstellung – distance setting
Entfernungsmesser – range-finder
entfesselte Kamera – living camera
entgegen dem Uhrzeigersinn – counter-clockwise
entmagnetisieren – to degauss, to demagnetize
Entschäumer – defoamer
Entwickler – developer
Entwicklung – development, developing, processing
Entwicklungsbedingungen – conditions of development

Entwicklungsdose – developing box
Entwicklungsmaschine – processor
Entwicklungsschale – developing dish
Entwicklungsspirale – reel
Entwicklungssubstanz – developing agent
Entwicklungstank – tank
Entwicklungszeit – duration of developing
entzerren – to unsqueeze
entzerren (beim Vergrößern) – to redress
Entzerrung – compensation of distortion
erden – to ground
Erdung – ground
erhöhen – to increase
Erstausstrahlung – first broadcasting
erste Arbeitsschicht – first unit
1. kombinierte Kopie – first trial composite
1. Korrekturkopie – first answer print
Erstentwickler – first developer
1. Beleuchtungsassistent – best boy
erster Entwurf – first draft
1. Kameraassistent – camera operator
1. Kameramann – director of photography
1. Tonassistent – sound recorder (US)
1. Schnittkopie – first answer print
1. Team – A-team
Erwähnung der Namen des technischen Stabes und der Darsteller auf dem Titelvorspann und im Programm – billing
Essenspause – meal period
Exklusivrechte – exclusive rights
Exposé – synopsis
extrahart – extra vigorous
exzentrische Blende – eccentric irising

F

Fachpresse – trade press
Fadenkreuz – cross hairs, graticle, reticle
Fahnen (bei Videokameras) – long streaking
Fahraufnahme – dollying shot, dollyshot, follow shot, traveling shot, tracking shot
fahrbares Studiostativ – pedestal
Fahrbereitschaft – motor pool
Fahrstativ – castered skid, rolling tripod, wheeled skid, wheeled tee, wheeled tie-down, wheeled triangle
Fahrzeug, das ein zu filmendes Fahrzeug (»target car«) zieht. Auf ihm sind Licht und Kamera montiert. – insert car
faltbare Augenmuschel – flexible eyecup
Faltlichtschachtsucher – waist level finder
Farbabgleich – color matching, matching
Farbabschwächer – dye reducer
Farbabweichung – color aberration, hue error
Farbanalyse – analysis of color
Farbauflösungsvermögen – acouity of color image, acuity of color definition, acuteness of color definition (US)
Farbauszug – chromatic selection
Farbbalkengeber – bar generator
Farbbild – color print
Farbdia – color slide
Farbdreieck – color triangle
Farbempfindlichkeit – chromatic sensitivity
Farbenrad – rainbow wheel
Farbentreue – color fidelity
Farbentwickler – color developer, dye coupling developer
Farbfehler – chromatical aberration
farbfehlerfrei – achromatic, achromatically
Farbfilm – color film
Farbfilterscheibe – color filter disk
Farbgleichgewicht – color balance
Farbhilfsträger – video sub carrier
Farbkoordinate – color coordinate

Farbkopf – color head
Farbkorrektur – color correction, color matching, matching
farbkorrigiert – color corrected
Farbkuppler – dye
Farbkupplungsentwickler – dye coupling developer
farblos – achromatic, achromatically
Farbluminanzsignal – Y-signal
Farbort der blauen Primärfarbe – blue apex
Farbregler – chroma control, color control, hue control, paint pots
Farbreinheit – color purity
Farbsaum – color fringing, chromatic fringe
Farbschablonentrick – chroma-key
farbstichig – tinged
Farbstoff – dye
Farbsynchronsignal – burst, color burst
Farbtemperatur – color temperature
Farbtestprobe – color cinex test
Farbteststreifen – test stripe
Farbton – chromaticity, hue
Farbtrennung – color separation
Färbung – shade
Farbverlust – fringing
Farbwechsel – allochroism
Farbwert – chrominance
Farbwertregler – chroma control, color control, hue control, paint pots
Farbzwischenpositiv – intermediate positive
Farmerscher Abschwächer – Farmer's reducer
Fassung – fitting
fazen – to kine
FBAS-Signal – composite signal
federnde Andruckplatte – spring pressure plate
Federwerkkamera – clockwork-motor camera
Fehlanpassung – mismatching
Fehlbesetzung – miscast
Feineinstellung – fine adjustment
Feinkornentwickler – fine-grain developer
Feinkörnigkeit – fine graininess
Feinkornkopie für Trickfilme – fine-grain print

Feinkornmaterial – fine-grain stock
Feinregler – fine tuning control
Feinschnitt – final cut, re-editing
Fensterprogramm – window program
Fernaufnahme – long distance view, vista shot
Fernbedienung – remote control
Fernrohrsucher – telescopic finder
Fernsehabtaster – scanner
Fernsehansager – video announcer
Fernsehanstalt – network, telecaster, TV broadcaster
Fernseharchiv – television archives
Fernsehaufnahmewagen – video bus, television cameratruck, TV reporting car
Fernsehausstrahlung eines Films – televising of a film
Fernsehbild – television tube image
Fernsehbild mit leichtem blau oder grün Stich – cool picture
Fernsehdrehbuch – TV shooting script
Fernseher – television receiver, television set
Fernsehintendant – television director
eine Fernsehkamera abgleichen – to set up the camera
Fernsehkanalumsetzer – TV frequency transposer, TV frequency converter
Fernsehnorm – television standard
Fernsehsender – video transmitter
Fernsehsendung – telecast
Fernsehsendung, die sich um junge Mädchen dreht – tits and asses
Fernsehspiel – teleplay, television drama
Fernsehtechnik – television engineering
Fernsehtechniker – video operator, video technican
Fernsehtestbild – television chart, television test cart
Fernsehübertragung – transmission
Fernsehzuschauer – video viewer
Festbrennweite, festbrennweitiges Objektiv – prime lens, fixed focal length lens
feste Bildeinstellung – fixed angle
Feststellen der Sehbeteiligung – rating
Feststellschrauben – adjusting knobs
Fettstift – chinagraph, chinagraph wax pencil, china marker
Feuchtigkeit – humidity, moisture

Film – flick, flicker (*slang*), motion-picture (US), movie, screen
einen Film drehen – to crank a film
einen Film mit Ton unterlegen – to dub in (the) sound
einen Film senden – to televise a film
»Film ab!«, Anweisung an den Kameramann – »Roll camera!«, »Roll!«, »Roll'em!«
Film abklammern – to clip
Filmablagerung – deposit of the film
Filmabsatz – deposit on the film
Filmabtaster – filmscanner, telecine, telecine machine
Filmanfang – head of the film
Filmarchitekt – art director, set builder
Filmarchivar – film librarian
Filmaufnahme – shot, take
Filmaufnahme ohne Ton – mute shot
Film aus dem Magazin auslegen – to unload
Filmausrüstung – film equipment
Filmausschnitt – footage
Filmbauten – setting of a feature
Filmbeschädigung – mutilation of film
Filmbesprechung – film review
Filmbespurung – sound track striping
Filmbetrachtungsgerät – film viewer
Filmbewertungsstelle – Film Assesment Board
Filmbild – film frame, frame
Filmbobby – core
Filmbobby mit 75mm (50mm) Durchmesser – Z core (T core)
Filmbreite – width of film
Filmbüchse – can
Filmbühne – negative carrier
Filmbunker – vault, vault storage for film
Filmbüro – filmservice
Film, der für Jugendliche ab 16 Jahren freigegeben ist – X-Certificate (GB)
Film, der nur für Jugendliche unter 16 Jahre freigegeben ist, wenn sie von einem Erwachsenen begleitet werden – R-rated
Film, der nur in den großen Kinos läuft – road show
Film, der ohne Zahlung von Lizenzgebühren aufgeführt oder gesendet

werden darf – public domain material
Film einlegen – to thread, to load
Filmempfindlichkeit – emulsion speed, grading, speed
Filmempfindlichkeit nach ASA – A.S.A. speed
filmen – to film, to shoot
Filmende – tail of the film
Filmentwicklungsmaschine – dip and dunk processor
Filmformat – film gauges
Filmgalgen – pin rack
Filmgeber – filmscanner, scanner
Filmgelände – studio lot
Filmhobel – scraper, splicer
Film im Kino anlaufen lassen – to open with a film
Filmindustrie – film industry (GB), motion picture industry (US)
Film in ein Magazin einlegen – to load, to load a camera, to thread
filmisch – filmic, filmically
Filmkamera – camera, cine-camera, Scherzwort: the Baby
Filmkarriere – film career (GB), movie career (US)
Filmkern – bob, core, film core
Filmkern mit 75mm (50mm) Durchmesser – Z core (T core)
Filmkitt – film cement
Filmklammer – film clip
Filmklappe – clapper, clapper board, scene slate, slate
Filmkleber – cement, film cement
Filmkommentar – commentary, narration, voice over
Filmkontinuität – continuity
Filmkopie mit Lichttonspur – composite print, married print (GB), synchronised print, comopt (*Codewort*)
Filmkopie mit Magnettonspur – combined print, married stripe, commag (*Codewort*)
Filmkopie mit Ton – synchronized print
Filmkopie mit Untertiteln – superimposed print
eine Filmkopie putzen – to polish out a copy
Filmlaufgeschwindigkeit – running speed
Filmmagazin – magazine, camera roll
Filmmaterial synchron anlegen – to synchronize two separate stripes of film
Filmmusik – score, film music

Filmpatrone – film cartridge
Filmprojektor – projector
Filmreiniger – film cleaner
Filmrest – cut-out, short end
Filmriß – breaking of the film, film-break
Filmsalat (*slang*) – film jam, spaghetti (*slang*)
Filmschaffende – film-makers, film technicians
Filmschaltwerk – film guide, film transport system
Filmschlaufe – buckle
Filmschnitt – cut, editing
Filmschrammen durch zu festes Aufwickeln der Filmrolle – cinch marks
Filmspule bei Kleinbildfilm – spool
Filmstudio – shooting studio, studio
eine Filmszene in Einstellungen auflösen – to cover a scene, to breakdown a scene
Filmteam – crew, team, unit
Filmtechniker – cinetechnician
filmtechnische Zeitung – cine-technical paper
Filmtext – commentary
Filmtitel – credits, credit title, main title
Filmtransportkurbel – wind-up crank
Filmtransportrolle – intermittent sprocket, sprocket drum, sprocket wheel
Filmumroller – film winder
Film- und Tonaufnahme gleichzeitig in der Kamera auf vorbespurtem Filmmaterial – single system
Filmunterlage – base
Filmvorführer – projectionist
Filmvorspann – front credits
Filmwechselsack – film changing bag
Filter – filter
Filter, daß die tiefen und hohen Tonfrequenzen abschneidet – roll-off filter
Filterdichte – filter density
Filterfaktor – filter factor
Filterfolienstanze – cutter for gelatin foil, filter foil punch
Filterhalter – filter holder
Filterrad – filter wheel
Fischaugenobjektiv – bugeye, fish eye lens

Fixfokusobjektiv – universal focus lens
Fixiersalz – fixing salt
Flächenleuchte – bank, bank of lamps
flau – blurred, without contrast
Fleck – stain
fließendes Wasser – running water
flimmerfrei – absence of flicker
flüssig – liquid
Fluter – basher
FM-Demodulation – demodulation of frequency modulation, rectification of frequency modulation
fokussieren – to focus, to pull focus, to ride focus, to throw focus
Fokussiergriff – quick-focusing handle
Formalinfixierbad – formalin fixer
Formatmaske – framing mask, matching format mask
Fotoalbum – photo album
Fotoarchiv – photo library, stills library
Fotochemikalien – photo chemicals
Fotodiode – photo-conductor
Fotoelement – photo-electric cell
fotogen – photogenic
Fotograf – photographer
Fotografie mit vorhandenem Licht – available light photography
fotografische Aufnahme, Schuß (*slang*) – shot, take
fotografische Chemikalien – photographic grade chemicals
fotografische Vergrößerung – blow-up
Fotogrammetrie – photogrammetry
Fotohändler – photo dealer
Fotokopiergerät – photocopier, photocopying apparatus
Fotolabor – lab, photographic laboratory
Fotomontage – composition photo
Fotopapier – photographic paper
Fotosatz – film-setting, photo-composition, photosetting
Fotowiderstand – photo-conductor
Fotozelle – photo-electric cell
Freiberufler – free lancer
Fremdquelleneinspeisung – mixed feeds
Fremdspannungsabstand – unweighted signal-to-noise ratio

fremdsprachliche Fassung eines Filmes – foreign version of a film
Frequenzbandbreite – width of the frequency band, white-to-black frequency deviation
Frequenzgang – amplitude-frequency response
Fresnelscheibe – fresnel screen
Friktion – brake of the film-run
frisches Bandmaterial – virgin
Frontaufheller – basher, camera light, camera headlamp, eyelight
Frontlinse – front glass
Frontprojektionsverfahren mit einer Scotchlite Leinwand – Scotchlite process
Froschperspektive – low-angle shot, worm's eye view
Führungslicht – key light
Füllsender – fill-in transmitter
Fundus – property department, stock
5kW Stufenlinse – senior
35mm Objektiv – 35mm lens
35mm Rohfilm – standard stock
Funkhaus – broadcasting house
Funkmikrofon – radio microphone, wireless microphone
Funksprechgerät – radio telephone
Fussel – deposit of the film, dirt, hair
Fusselkontrolle des Filmfensters – to check the gate, hair-check
Fußnummern (Meternummer) – footage-number
Fußschalter – foot commutator

G

Gage – fee, salary
Galgen (*slang*), **Mikrofonkran** – boom
Gammawert – gamma value
Gang mit der Handkamera – running shot
Ganzmetallgehäuse – all-metal box
Garderobe – dressing-room (GB), checkroom (US)
Gazeschirm – scrim
gebogene Schiene – curved rail
gefilmtes Fahrzeug. Wird vom »insert car« gezogen – target car
Gegenlicht (außen) – backlight
Gegenlicht (innen) – kick-light, rim-light
Gegenlichtbeleuchtungstechnik – low key
Gegenschuß – direct reverse, reaction shot (~ angle, ~ shot)
Gegensprechleitung – talkback circuit, talkback line
Gegentaktverstärker – push-pull amplifier
Geisterbild – multi path effect (US)
Gelatinefilter – jelly
Gelb – yellow
gelbstichig – yellow tinged
gelöschtes Band – clean tape
gelungene Aufnahme – hold take, succeedet shot
Generalprobe – dress rehersal
gerade Schiene – straight rail
Geräuschband – effects track, sound effects tape
Geräusche – sound effects
Geräuschemacher – sound effect technican, effects operator
geringe Verzeichnung – low distortion
Gesamtansicht, Gesamtaufnahme – total view, vista shot
Geschichte – story
Geschichte eines Film – film story, plot
geschlossene Vorstellung – private performance
geschnittene Arbeitskopie – cutting copy
Geschwindigkeit – velocity
Gesichtsfarbe – flesh tone
Gesichtsfeld – camera coverage

»**Gestorben!**« (*slang*), **akzeptierte Aufnahme** – »Wrap!«, »It's a wrap!«
Gewerkschaft – trade union, union
Gitter – grid
Gitterspannung – bias
Glasfaserkabel – optical fibre
Glühbirne – bulb
Glühlampe – globe
Grauempfindung – achromatic sensation
Graukeil – grey scale
Grauverhältnis – tonal proportions
Greifersystem – film guide, film transport system
Großformatkamera, Studiokamera (Foto) – large size camera, view camera
größte Totale innerhalb einer Sequenz – master shot
Gummilinse (*slang*) – zoom lens
Gummispinne – rubber spider

H

halbdurchlässiger Spiegel – half silvered mirror, one-way mirror, surface mirror, transparent mirror
halbe Drahtgaze – half scrim
1/2kW Lampe – baby spot, pup
Halbleiter – semiconductor
Halbleiterfotoschicht-Kameraröhre – photo conducting camera tube
Halbnahe – semi close-up
Halbnaheinstellung – two-shot, medium shot
Halbschatten – half-shade
Halbtotale – close medium shot, medium long shot, mid shot
Halbwelle – half-sine wave
hallig – reverberant
Hallplatte – reverberation plate, echo plate
Hallraum – echo chamber
Halogenlicht – quarz-light
Halogensilber – silver halide
Handbuch – instruction manual, manual
Handkamera – hand camera, portable camera
Handlampe – hand-held lamp, hand-held light
Handlung eines Film – film story, plot
Handregelmotor – variable speed motor, wild motor
Handschlaufe – wrist strap
Handsprechfunkgerät – walkie-talkie
Härtebad – hardener, hardening solution
Härtefixierbad – hardening fixing bath
Härtestopbad – hardener stop bath
Hartgummi – hard rubber
Hartschnittumschalter – video switch
hart überblenden – to cut
Hartzeichnerobjektiv – high-definition lens
Hauptdarsteller – feature player, headline, lead, leading actor, top-player
Hauptfilm – full length film
Hauptprobe – dress run
Hauptrolle – leading part
Hauptschalter – main switch

Hauptsendezeit – prime time
Haupttitel – main title
Heimkino – home movies
heiße Probe – dry run
Heißklebepresse – hot splicer
heizbare Augenmuschel – heatable eyecup
hell – light
heller Sucher – bright view-finder
Helligkeitsgradation – key
Helligkeitskontrast – brightness contrast
Helligkeitsumfang – key
Hellsteuerimpuls – indicator gate
herausbringen – to present
Herstellungskosten – production cost
Hertz – cps, cycles per second
herunter kopieren – to reduce optical
HI Lampe – brute
Hilfskraft – best boy
Hilfslinse – additional lens
Hilfsspiegel – additional mirror
Hilfsstandarte – intermediate standard
Hilfsträger – subcarrier
Hilfsträgerfrequenz – subcarrier frequency
Hilfsträgerphase des Farbsynchronsignals – burst phase
H-Impuls – line pulse, line synchronisation impulse
Hinterbandkontrolle beim Tonbandgerät – headset monitoring
hinterer Objektivdeckel – rear lens cap
hintere Standarte – back standard
Hintergrund – background, backing
Hintergrund (sowohl natürlicher bei Außenaufnahmen als auch künstlicher bei Studioaufnahmen) – scenery
Hintergrundgemälde – mural
Hintergrundgeräusche in einer Massenszene – walla-walla
Hintergrundmusik – under
Hinweisschild vor Studios: »Drehort nicht betreten!« – »Closed set!«
historischer Film – costume film
Hoch/Tiefverschiebung – vertical shift
hochauflösendes Objektiv – high-definition lens

hochempfindlicher Film – fast film, high-speed film
Hochformataufnahme – vertex picture
Hochfrequenz – radio frequency
Hochfrequenzkinematografie – high-speed cinematography
Hochglanzfoto – glossy
Hochglanzpapier – glazed paper
Hochlaufzeit – pre-roll time, run-up time
Hochtonlautsprecher – high frequency loudspeaker, tweeter (US)
hochzeilige hohe Auflösung – high definition, high resolution
Höhe der Leinwand – screen height
Höhen – treble
Höhenabsenkung – treble cut
Höhenanhebung – treble boost
hohe Plattform – high-stand
hoher Ton – high pitched sound
hohes Lampenstativ – highroller
Hohlkehle – cove, ground cove, merging curve
Hohlspiegel – concave mirror reflector
Holografie – holography
Hologramm – hologram
Holzstativ – wooden tripod
Honorar – salary
hörbarer Frequenzbereich – audible frequency
hörbare Verzerrung – audible distortion
Hörbarkeitsschwelle – threshold of audibility
Hörfunkreportage – radio OB
(horizontaler) Schneidetisch – flatbed
horizontaler Schneidetisch – flat bed editing machine
horizontal schwenken – to pan
Hörkopf – pick-up head, playback head
Hornhaut (Auge) – cornea
Horrorfilm – spooky movie (*slang*)
Hörschwelle – minimum audible field
Hör-Sprech-Kombination – headset
Hubschrauberaufhängung – helicopter mount, Tyler mount
180° Schwenk der Kamera – roundy round
100kW Scheinwerfer – big eye
100% Aussteuerung – full modulation

100W oder 200 W Spotscheinwerfer – dinky-inky
110° Farbbildröhre – color picture tube of 110°
120m Kassette – 400 foot magazine
Hydroantrieb – fluid drive
Hydrokopf – fluid head

I

Idee des Regisseurs, ein Drehbuch umzusetzen – director's plan for covering a scene
Ikonoskop – iconoscope
im Blickfeld der Kamera – in camera
im Blickfeld der Kamera – in camera
Impuls – pulse
im vorderen Teil der Bühne – downstage
im vorderen Teil der Bühne – downstage
in der Bewegung schneiden – to cut on move, to cut on action
in der Bewegung schneiden – to cut on move, to cut on action
indirektes Licht – bounced light
indizierter Film – banned film, X-rated film (GB)
Induktivität – inductivity
Infrarot – infra-red
Infrarotbildwandler – infra-red image converter
Infrarotfarbfilm – color infra-red film
Infrarotvidikon – infra-red vidicon
Inhalt eines Film – film story, plot
Inhaltsangabe – plot
Inhaltsverzeichnis – index
Innenaufnahme – indoor shot
Innenfokussierung – internal focusing
Innenrequisiteur – property man
Innenwiderstand – interval resistance
in Richtung der Kamera – down stage
in Richtung der Kamera – down stage
ins Bild kommen – to come into shot
ins Bild kommen – to come into shot
Inserat – advertisement, publicity
Inspezient – stage manager
inszenieren – to direct
Inszenierung eines Films – realization of a feature
Intendant – director
Interessentenvorführung – trade show
Interferenz – beat

Interkom – intercom, party line
internationales Tonband – music and effects track
Irisblende – iris diaphragm
Italo-Western – spaghetti western
IT-Band – M & E track
IT-Fassung – M & E version

J

Jaulen – wow
jede Art von Fahrzeug, das von Komparsen verwendet wird – atmosphere vehicle
Journalist – journalist, reporter
Jury – jury
justieren – adjust
Justierschraube – adjusting screw
Justitiar – justiciary, legal adviser

K

Kabel – cable
Kabelanschluß – cable reception
Kabelfernsehkunde – subscriber
Kabelhilfe – cable grip, cableman, cable person, cable puller
Kabelkanal – cable duct
Kabellängenausgleich – cable correction, cable length compensation, cable length equilisation
Kabelsalat – set of wires
Kabeltrommel – cable reel
Kalibrierung – calibration
Kalkulation – budget
Kalkulationsformular – budget form
Kalkulationsposten – budget line items
Kalkulationsschema – budget outline
kalte Farben – cool colors
Kaltlaminiergerät – pressure-sensitive laminator
Kamera – camera, cine-camera, movie camera
»Kamera ab!«, Anweisung an den Kameramann – »Turn over!«
Kameraabgleich – camera set-up
Kameraassistent – assistant cameraman, focus puller, focus operator
Kameraassistent (der die Klappen schlägt) – clapperboy
Kamerafahrt mit Dolly – dollying shot, dollyshot, follow shot, traveling shot, tracking shot
Kamerafilm – color master
Kameragehäuse – body, camera body
Kameragewichtsausgleich – camera balancing
Kamerakran – camera boom, camera crane
Kameramann – cameraman, operating cameraman
Kamera mit einem Bajonettanschluß anstatt eines Revolvers – hard-front camera
Kamera mit Federwerkmotor – clockwork-motor camera
Kameraneiger – tilt head, tilting head, tilting platform, tilt top, tiltop
Kameraobjektiv – taking lens
Kamera- oder Mikrofonkran – boom
die Kamera abgleichen – to set up the camera

Kameraröhren durch Abdecken vor Lichteinfall schützen – capping-up
Kameraschwenkung – panning
Kamerastandort – set
Kamerawagen – dolly, trolly
Kamerawinkel – camera angle
Kanalabstand – channel spacing
Kanalumsetzer – channel conversion
Kanalwähler – tuner
Kanalweiche – channel combining unit diplexer
Kanone (*slang*), **Richtmikrofon** – shot gun, unidirectional microphone
Kantenschärfe – corner detail
Kantine – cafeteria, commissary, lunchroom (US), snackbar
Kapellmeister – conductor, musical director (GB)
Kasch – cash, matte, mask, vignette
Kassenrekord – box-office record
Kassette – magazine
Kassettenschieber – locking dark slide
Kassettentasche – magazine pouch
Kassettenwechselsack – changing bag
Kathodenstrahlröhre – cathode-ray tube
Kaufvertrag – sales agreement, sales contract
Kehrbild – image upside down
Keilentfernungsmesser – wedge range-finder
Kennlinienknick – rupture in characteristic curve
Kerbmarkierung – code notch
Kino – movie
Kinofilm – motion picture film
Kinogänger – moviegoer
Kinokarte – ticket
Kinoneiger – tilting head, tilting platform, tilt top, tiltop
Kinotechnik – cinema technics
Kinowerbung – cinema advertising
Kintopp (*slang*) – flicks, flicker, vintage movie
Kippablenkung – time base
Kippfrequenz – sweep frequency
Kippgenerator – sweep generator, sweep oszillator, timebase generator
Kippschaltung – sweep voltage, timebase voltage
Kissenverzeichnung – pincushion distortion

»K«, »Kopierer«, Bemerkung im Negativbericht – »P«., »Print«
Klammermaterial – paper-to-paper
Klammerteil – film clip
Klangfarbe – timbre, tone color
Klappe – camera marker, clapp stick, clapper board, scene slate, slate
»Klappe schlagen!«, »Bitte die Klappe!«, Anweisung an den Assistenten – »Mark it!«
Klappkamera – folding camera
Klappstativ – telescopic floor stand
Klärbad – clearing bath, clarifying bath
Klarglasscheibe – plain glass screen
Klatsche (*slang*) – dailies (US), rush (GB), rushes (GB), rush print (GB), working print, work print
Klebeband – foil, gaffer tape, sealing tape
Klebelade, Klebepresse – film joiner, film splicer
Klebepresse für Bild- und Tonschnitt – tape splicer with double side cutter
Kleberin – editing girl, splicing girl
Klebestellengeräusch – bloop, splice bump
Klebetisch – editing table
klebrig – tacky
Kleindarsteller – bit player, walk on 2
kleine Lichtblende – dot
kleiner Kamerawagen – doorway dolly
kleiner Ü-Wagen – car for reportage and topicals, window unit
Klemme – grid-clip
Klemmschuh – T-shoe
Klirrfaktor – distortion, distortion factor, distortion percentage
Kniff – gimmick
knochig (*slang*)**, zu kontrastreich** – too contrasty, snoot and white wash (*slang*)
Koaxialkabel – co-axial cable
die Köpfe einmessen – to align the heads, heads alignment
Koffer – carrying case
Kohlebogen – carbon arcs
Kollimator – collimator
Koma – coma
kombinierter Aufnahme-Wiedergabekopf – combined recording-reproducing head

komischer Film – comical film
Kommentar – commentary, narration, voice over
Komödie – comedy, farce
Komparse – extra, super, supernumerary, walk on 1
Komparsengage – walk-on fee
Kompatibilität – compatibility
Kompendium – lens hood, matte box
komplementärer Farbton – complementary hue
Komplementärfarbe – complementary color
Komponist – composer
Kompressor – speech processor
Kondensor – condensing lens, condensor
Kondensorlinse – condensor lens
konkav – concave
konkav-konvex – concavo-convex
konkav-konvex Linse – concavo-convex lens
Kontaktkopie – contact print, direct print
Kontaktkopiermaschine – contact printer
Kontrast – contrast
kontrarm – contrasty
Kontrastabfall – low contrast
Kontrastfaktor – contrast factor
Kontrastfilter – contrast filter
Kontrastglas – pan glas, viewing filter
kontrastlos – blurred
Kontrastregler – shader
kontrastreich – contrasty, hard, high contrast
Kontrastumfang – brightness range, range of contrast
Kontrollampe – pilot lamp
Kontrollautsprecher – monitor loudspeaker
Kontrollmonitor – line monitor
Kontrolloszilloskop – wave form monitor
Kontrollstreifen – control strip
Konturenschärfe – acutance, apparent sharpness, contour sharpness
Konvergenz – convergence
Konvergenztestbild – grille
Konversionsfilter (Kunstlicht auf Tageslicht) – macbeth
konvex – convex
Kopfabrieb – head wear

Kopfaufnahme – head shot
Kopfhörer – can, earphone, head band
Kopfhörer-Mikrofon-Kombination – headset
Kopflicht – basher, camera light, camera headlamp, eyelight
Kopfträger – head-support assembly
Kopie – copy
Kopienkontrolle – film inspection
Kopienziehen – to print, to make a print
kopieren – to print
»Kopieren!«, Anweisung an das Scriptgirl – »Print it!«, »Save it!«
»Kopierer«, Bemerkung im Negativbericht – »P.«, Print!
Kopierfilm – print film
Kopierfilmmaterial – print stock
Kopierlänge – printing length
Kopierlicht – printer light, printing light, timing light
Kopiermaschine – printing machine
Kopiermeister – filmgrader
Kopierstraße für n-Bänder – dubber for n-tapes
Kopierverfahren – printing process
Kopierverlust – printing loss
Kopierwerk – film processing works, lab, laboratory, laboratory for processing
Kopierwerksarbeiten – film processing works
Kopierwerksbericht – lab report
Kopierwerksblende – printer fade
Koproduktion – co-production
Koproduzent – co-producer
Korbwindschutz – basked windshield, zeppelin, zeppelin windscreen
Korn – grain
Korndichte – grain density
Korngröße – grain size
Körnigkeit – graininess
Körperschall – structure-born vibration
korrekte Belichtung – correct exposure
Korrekturfahne – page proof
Korrekturkopie – first release print, graded print (GB), timed print (US)
Korrekturlinse – correcting lens
Kostenvoranschlag – budget breakdown

Kostümberater – costume adviser, stylist, wardrobe supervisor (GB)
Kostümentwurf – costume design
Kostümfundus – wardrobe
Kostümrequisite – dressing props
Kostümverleih – costume house
Kraftverstärker – booster amplifier, main ~, power ~
Kran – crane
Kranfahrer – crane operator
Kratzer – scratch
Kratzer auf dem Film – cinch marks
Kreiselkopf – gyroscopic head, gyro head
Kreiselstativ – gyro-tripod
Kreisfahrt – arc shot
Kreuzdipol – crossed dipole, turnstile aerial
Kriegsfilm – war film
Kriminalfilm – detective film, mystery play
Kristallmikrofon – piezoelectric microphone
Kristalltonabnehmer – crystal pick-up
Kritik – review
Kritiker – reviewer
Krokodilklemme – alligator grip, alligator cramp, bear trap, crocodile clip, gaffer grip, gaffer cramp, gator grip
Kronglas – crown glass
Krümmungsradius – radius of curvature
Kugelgelenkkopf – ball-and-socket head
Kugelschale – head bowl
Kugelschwenk- und Neigekopf – friction pan-and-tilt head
kühl – cool
Kühlschrank – refrigerator
Kühlung – cooling
Kulisse – wing
Kulturfilm – cultural film
Kulturredakteur – arts feature editor, cultural affairs editor
Kundendiensttechniker im Außendienst – home technician
Künstler – artist
Künstlervertrag – artist's contract
Künstleragentur – talent agency
Künstlergarderobe – artist's dressing-room

künstlerische Oberleitung – supervision
künstliche Alterung – artificial aging
Kunstlicht – artificial light
Kunstschnee – snow effect
kürzen – to cut, to cut back, to trim
Kunstlichtaufnahme – artificial-light shot
Kurbel – crank
kurbeln – to crank
Kurierdienst – courier service
Kurzfassung – synopsis
Kurzfilm – art film, film on art, short film, short
Kurzmeldung – news flash
Kurznachrichten – news brief
Kurzschluß – short-circuit
Kurzzeitbelichtung – short time exposure

L

Ladegerät – charger
Ladungsbild – charge image (GB), image pattern (US)
Lagerung – storage
Laminieren – laminating
Lampe, die sichtbar in der Dekoration steht – practical lamp
Lampen aufbauen – to rig the lamps
Lampen einschalten – to hit the lights, to give the lamps the juice (*slang*)
Lampenstativ – telescopic floor stand
Lampentor – barn door
Lampenwechsel – lamp replacement
Landschaftsfotografie – landscape photography
langbrennweitig – long-focus
langbrennweitiges Zoomobjektiv – telephoto range zoom lens
langsamer Rolltitel – crawl title
Langwelle – long waves
Lassoband – adhesive tape, clothtape, gaffer tape (*slang*)
Lasurfarbe – transparent color
latent – latent
Laufbildbetrachter – animated viewer, film viewer, viewer
Laufbodenkamera – baseboard camera, flatbed view camera
Laufgeräusch der Filmkamera – camera noise
»Läuft!« – »Running!«
Laufwerk – tape drive
Laufzeit – length of a scene, timing
Laufzeit eines Films – running time
Lautsprecher – loudhailer (GB)
Lautstärke – volume
Lautstärkeregler – volume control
Lavaliermikrofon – lanyard microphone, lavalier microphone, personal microphone
Lavendelkopie – fine grain master
Leerband – virgin tape
Lehre vom Schall – acoustics
Lehrfilm – film course
Leichtdolly – light dolly

leichte Unschärfe (auch als künstlerischer Effekt) – soft focus
Leichtkompendium – lightweight matte box
Leinwand – screen
Leinwandgröße – screen size
Leinwandhöhe – screen height
Leinwandkasch – cover frame of the screen
Leiste zum Aufhängen von Lampen – batten
Leistungsaufnahme – power consumption
Leistungsnachweis – proof of performance
Leistungsverstärker – booster amplifier, main amplifier, power amplifier
Leistungsverstärkung – power amplification
leitender Filmarchitekt – supervising set builder
Leiter – conductor
Leiter der Fahrbereitschaft – driver foreman
Leitungsabschluß – line termination, circuit termination
Lektor – reader
Lektorat – story department
Lesebereich – reading time
Lesefehler – reading error
letzte Einstellung eines Drehtags – Abby singer shot (*slang*)
Leuchte – flood light
Leuchtrahmensucher – illuminated frame finder
Leuchtstoff – luminophor
Leuchtstoffröhre – fluorescent tube
»Licht aus!« Anweisung an die Beleuchter – »Save the arcs!«, »Save the lights!«
Lichtabteilung – electric department
Lichtausrüstung – lighting equipment
lichtbestimmte Kopie – balanced print, timed print
Lichtbestimmung – direction of lighting, grading, timing of printing light, timing of print light
Lichtblende – flag
Lichtbogen – luminous arc
Licht bündeln – to bunch the light
Lichteinfall – light leak, light struck
Lichteinfallwinkel – field angle
Lichteinwirkung – action of light
lichtelektrische Zelle – photo conductor
lichtempfindlich – sensitive to light

Lichtempfindlichkeit – luminous sensitivity
Lichter – highlights
Lichtfilter – light filter
Lichtführung – direction of lighting
Lichthof – halo
lichthoffrei – anti-halo
Lichthofschutz – antihalation
Lichthofschutzschicht – antihalation backing, antihalation layer
Lichtkasten – light box
Lichtkegel – cone
Lichtpausapparat – blue-printing frame
Lichtpause – blue-print
Lichtpauspapier – blue-print paper
Lichtpunktabtaster – flying spot scanner
Lichtquelle – light source
Lichtschachtsucher – focusing hood
Lichtschleuse – light trap
lichtschluckend – light absorbing
Lichtschutz – french flag
Licht setzen – reflector direction
lichtsetzender Kameramann – director of photography
Lichtsignal – light signal
Lichtstärke eines Objektivs – lens speed, maximum aperture, speed
lichtstarkes Objektiv – fast lens, high-speed objective
Lichtstativ – lighting stand
Lichtstrahl – ray of light
Lichtton – optical sound
Lichttonkamera – film sound recorder
Lichttonkamera für Sprossenschrift – density recorder
Lichttonsprossenschrift – variable density recording
Lichttonzackenschrift – variable area track
lichtundurchlässig – light-tight
Lichtverlust – loss of light
Lichtwanne – lighting float, broad source, broad
Lichtwert – exposure value
Liebhaber – lover
Lieferbedingungen – conditions of delivery
Lifesendung – life transmission

Linearität – linearity
linke Bühnenseite – stage left
Linse – lens
Linsenglied – lens element
Linsenvergütung – lens coating
Linsenverkittung – cementing of lenses
lippensynchron – lip-sync
Liste der Einstellungen für den E-Schwenker – shot sheet
literarische Umsetzung eines films – novelization
live ohne üben – ad lip
Lochmaske – aperture mask
Löschdrossel – bulk eraser
löschen – to erase
löschen von Magnetbändern – to wipe
Löschkopf – erasing head
Lösung – solution
Lösung ansetzen – to mix
löten – to solder
Lötkolben – copper bit, copper bolt, soldering iron
Lotrechte – vertical-line
Lötstelle – soldering joint
Lötverbindung – soldering connexion
low-budget Film – B-movie, low-budget film
Luftaufnahme – aerial photography
Luftbild – aerial view
Luftbildkamera – aerial camera
luftdichte Metallbüchse – air-tight metal box
Luftfeuchtigkeit – humidity
Luftfracht – air-freight
Luft-Glas Grenzfläche – air-glass interface
Luft-Luftaufnahme – air-to-air shot
Luftspalt (im Magnettonkopf) – air gap (in the magnetic head)
Lumanz – luminance
Lumineszenz – luminescence
Lupe – magnifier, magnifying glass
Lux – footcandle
Lux-Meter – incident light meter

M

Madenschraube – grub screw, headless screw
Magazindeckel – magazine lid
Magazinschieber – magazine slide
Magazinverriegelung – magazine locking mechanism
Magnetausgleichsspur auf Filmkopien – balance stripe
Magnetbespurung eines Films durch Aufgiessen der Tonspur – magnetic striping
Magnetbespurung eines Films durch Aufkleben der Tonspur – magnetic laminating
magnetisches Wechselfeld – alternating magnetic field
Makrohebel – macro switch
Malteserkreuz – crosswheel, Geneva stop, Maltese cross
Malteserkreuzgetriebe – Geneva motion, Geneva movement, Maltese cross assembly
Mantel-und-Degen-Film – spectacle picture
manuelle Blende – manual diaphragm
Markierung – cue mark
Maske – mask, vignette, vor Scheinwerfern: cookie, cucaloris
Maskenbildner – make-up man
Maskenbildnerassistent – make-up assistant
Masken-Farbbildröhre – shadow mask tube
Maske vor Scheinwerfern, um Schatten zu erzeugen – cookie, cucaloris
Maskierung – masking
Maßband – tape
Masse – ground
Massenkopie – release print
Maßstab – plotting scale
Materialassistent – film loader
Materialfehler – material-defect
mattes Papier – dull-finish paper, dull-surfaced paper, mat paper
Mattscheibe – ground-glass, ground-glass disk, ground-glass screen, diffusing screen, focusing screen
Mattscheibe mit Mikroprismen – focusing screen with central grid
Mattscheibe mit Mikroprismen und Schnittbildentfernungsmesser – focusing screen with central grid and split-image range-finder
Mattscheibe mit Normalfilmformat-Markierung – academy format ground glass

Mattscheibe mit Schnittbildentfernungsmesser – focusing screen with split-image range-finder
Mattspray – dulling spray
»Mäusezähnchen-Effekt«, Bildzittern – jitter
maximaler Schwarzwert – black peak (US), peak black (GB)
Maximalwert – maximum value
MAZ-Wagen – van
mechanische Verschlußzeit – mechanical shutter speed
Megahertz – mega cycle
Mehrfachbelichtung – multiple exposure
Mehrfachentspiegelung – multicoating
Mehrfachgreifer – multiple claw
Mehrfachsteckdose – junction box, distribution box, plugging box, spider box
mehr Stimme geben – to give more voice
Meniskuslinse – concavo-convex lens
Meßbereich – measuring range
Meßfeld – acceptance angle
Meßfilm – calibration reel
Meßsignal – test signal
Messung der Sehbeteiligung – audience rating
Metallgehäuse – all-metal box
Metermaß – tape
Meterskala – meter scale
Meterzähler – footage counter
Mikrofilmstreifen – micro strip
Mikrofonangel – hand boom
Mikrofonaufstellung – position of microphone
Mikrofon für Nahbesprechung – close-talking microphone, lip microphone, noise cancelling microphone
Mikrofonhalterung – cradle suspension
Mikrofonkran, Mikrofongalgen (*slang*) – boom
Mikrofonwindschutz – wind gag
Mikrofotografie – microphotography
Mikroskopadapter – microscope adapter
Mikrotubus – micro-tube
Milchglas – glass porcelain
Mindesthelligkeit – minimum brightness
Mischband – mixed tracks, re-recorded reel
mischen – to mix

Mischpult – mixing desk
Mischpulteingang – channel
Mischpultverstärker – mixing amplifier
Mischung – re-recording
Mitautor – co-author
Mithörschalter – tape monitor switch
mit Playback Ton drehen – to shoot the playback
mit Playback Ton drehen – to shoot the playback
Mittelformatkamera – medium-format camera
Mittelwert – average value, mean value
mit Video aufnehmen – videotaping
mit Video aufnehmen – videotaping
Modellaufnahme – model shot
Moderator – anchor man, discussion chairman, moderator (US), presenter
moderieren – to present
Modulation – modulation
Modulationstiefe – modulation stage
Modulationsübertragungsfunktion – modulation transfer function
Moiré Effekt – Moiré effect, watered silk
Molton – Duvatyne, black drapping material
Momentverschluß – instantaneous shutter
Monitorlautsprecher – listening box
Monitorlautsprecher im Abhörraum – monitor loudspeaker, monitoring loudspeaker
monochromatisch – homogeneous
Montage – editing
montieren – to edit
Monumentalfilm – film on a vast scale
Motiv – location, set
Motivsuche – lining-up
Motivsucher – directors view-finder
Motor mit variabler Geschwindigkeit – variable speed motor, wild motor
musikalisches Thema – musical leitmotif
Musikband – music tape, music track
Musikkassette – musicassette
Muster, Musterkopie – dailies (US), rush (GB), picture daily print, rushes (GB), rush print (GB)
Muster trennen – break-down of rushes
Mustervorführung – screening of the rushes
Mutterband – master copy, master tape

N

Nachbarbildträger – adjacent picture carrier, adjacent vision carrier
Nachbarkanal – adjacent channel
Nachbild der Fernsehkamera – burned-in image, retained image, sticking picture
nach einer Erzählung von ... – based on a story by ...
Nachentwicklung – re-development
Nachführbelichtungsmesser – follow-pointer exposure meter
Nachführzeiger – coincidence adjusting pointer, moving adjusting pointer
Nachfüllösung – replenisher
nachgeführtes Führungslicht – travelling key
Nachhall – sound reverberation
Nachhallzeit – reverberation time
Nachleuchtcharakteristik einer Kathodenstrahlröhre – cathode-ray tube persistence characteristic
Nachleuchteffekt – persistence of vision
Nachleuchten – after glow, persistence, phosphorescence
Nachrichten – newscast
Nachrichtensprecher – newscaster, newsmaster
Nachspann – credits, credit titles, end credits
Nachsynchronisation in eine Fremdsprache – dubbing in a foreign language, language dubbing, post-dubbing
nachsynchronisieren – to dub, to postsynchronize
Nacht – night
Nachtaufnahme – night shot
Nachtdreh – night shot
Nachtvorstellung – night performance
Nachtzuschlag – night premium
Nachwuchs – young artists
Nachzieheffekt bei Videokameras – long streaking
Nachziehen – after-image, smearing effect
Nahaufnahme – close up (CU), tight shot
Naheinstellgerät – close-up focusing device
Naheinstellung – close range
Nahlinse – diopter, diopter lens
Nahpunkt – near limit, near point
Nahpunkt eines Objektivs – minimum focusing distance
naß – wet

Naßkopierfenster – wet gate
Nebel – fog
Nebelmaschine – fog machine, smoke gun
Nebenbild – secondary image
Nebendarsteller – supporting player
Nebenhandlung – secondary action, sub-plot
Nebenrolle – supporting part
Nebenträger – subcarrier
Negativ – negative
Negativ abziehen – to cut the negative
Negativabzieher (in) – negative cutter
Negativbericht – camera sheets, dope sheet, picture negative report
Negativ-Bild-Dup – picture dup-negative
Negativbühne – negative carrier, negative platform, negative stage
Negativfilm – negative material
Negativfussel – dirt in the gate
Negativretusche – negative retouching
Negativtaschen – storing pocket for negatives
Negativverstärkung – re-development
Neger – cue cards, idiot cards
Neger (*slang*) – cheese-cutter, gobo, meat axe, french flag
Neigekopf – tilt head, tilting head, tilting platform, tilt top, tiltop
neigen – to tilt
Neigung (einer Kamera) – tilting
Nennfrequenz – nominal frequency
Nennleistung – rated power output
Netzanschluß – net feeding, power supply
Netzbrummen – a.c. pickup, motor boating
Netzeingang – a.c. input
Netzgerät – a.c. power supply
Netzkabel – a.c. main lead
Netzspannungsschwankung – line voltage fluctuation
Netzstörung – net trouble
Netzteil – supply unit
neu einleuchten – to re-light
Neuinszenierung eines Films – remake
Neuproduktion – remake
neutraler Farbton – neutral hue
neutralgrau – neutral grey

Neutralisierbad – neutralizer
Neuverfilmung – remake
Newtonscher Ring – Newton effect
n-fache Vergrößerung – n-power magnification
NF-Filter – A.F. filter
NF-Verstärker – A.F. amplifier
nicht freigegebener Film – banned film
nicht im Bildfeld – out-of-frame
Nichtleiter – non-conductor
Nichtlinearität – non-linearity
nicht senden – to be off the air
Niederfrequenz – low frequency
Niederfrequenzverstärker – A.F. amplifier
Niedervolthalogenlampe – low voltage halogen lamp
Niedervoltlampe – low voltage lamp
Nipkowscheibe – aperture disk
Nitrofilm – nitrate film, nitrate base film
Nivellierplatte – balance plate, sliding base plate
Nivellierschlitten – levelling
»NK«, im Negativbericht für »nicht kopieren« – »NP«
normale, nicht anamorphotisch gepreßte Filmkopie – flat print
Normalfilmkamera – camera for standard film
Normalfilmkameraobjektiv – lens for standard film camera
Normalfrequenz – standard frequency
Normwandler – standards conversion equipment, standards converter, television system converter
Notausschalter – cut-out switch
Notiz – notation
Notstromaggregat – emergency generator
Nuance – shade
Nullage – zero position
Nulleinstellung – zero adjustment
Nulleiter – neutral wire
Nullkopie – answer print, approval ~, corrected ~, grading ~
Nullkopie ohne Lichtton – black track print
nur Ton – sound only
auf Null stellen – to zero out
Nutzleistung – useful power
Nutzton – signal

Oberbeleuchter – chief electrician, head electrician, gaffer
obere Filmschleife – top loop, upper film loop
Oberflächenhärtung – case-hardening
Oberlicht – overhead lighting
Objektiv – lens
Objektiv, lichtstark – fast lens
Objektivanschlußring – lens mounting ring
Objektivbeutel – lens pouch
Objektivblende – anterior shutter
Objektivbühne (bei Großformatkameras) – lensboard adapter
Objektivebene – lens plane
Objektivfassung – lens mount
Objektiv für 35mm Film – 35mm lens
Objektivhalter – lens flange
Objektiv mit fester Brennweite – prime lens, fixed focal length lens
Objektiv mit verkitteten Linsen – cemented lenses
Objektiv mit vorgesetztem Polfilter – polarized lens
Objektivöffnung – lens-aperture
Objektivrevolver – lens turret, turret head
Objektivsatz – set of lenses
Objektivschallschutz – zoom blimp
Objektivstandarte – lens panel, lens standard
Objektivstütze – lens support
Objektivträger – front standard assembly
Objektweite – object distance
off (*slang*), **off-Ton** – sound only
Offline-Schnitt – off-line editing
Offline-Schnittplatz – off-line suite
off-Text – voice over
öffentliche Vorführung – official presentation, public showing
Öffentlichkeitsarbeit – publicity
Öffnungsverhältnis – relative aperture
Ohmsches Gesetz – Ohm's law
Okular – eyepiece
Omega-Bandführung – omega loop, omega wrap

Opalglas – bone-glass
Opazität – opacity
optimales Sehvermögen – 20/20, best view
Option – first call, option
optische Achse – lens axis, optical axis, principal axis
optische Bank – Goerz attachment
optische Bankkamera – mono rail camera, optical bench camera
optische Blende – fade, printer fade
optische Effekte – optical effects, opticals
optische Kamerafahrt – to zoom
optischer Strahlenteiler – beam splitter
optischer Sucher – optical view-finder
optisches kopieren – optical printing
optisches Relaissystem – relay optics
optische Vergrößerung – blow-up
optische Verkleinerung – optical reduction
Orginalfarbfilm, der durch die Kamera lief – color master
Originalfassung – original version
Originalmaterial – camera original
Originalnegativ – original negative
Orthikon – orthicon
O-Ton – original sound, sync sound
Overlay-Trickmischung – moving matte, overlay, self-keyed insertion

P

panchromatisch – panchromatic
panchromatischer Schwarzweißfilm – panchromatic stock
Panoramaaufnahme – panoramic shot
Panoramaleinwand – panoramic screen
Panoramaregler – panpot
Panoramaschwenk – pan shot, panning shot
Pantograf, um Scheinwerfer zu aufgehängen – blanket rig
Parabolantenne – parabolic antenna
Parabolspiegel – parabolic mirror
Parallaxe – parallax
Parallaxenausgleich – compensation of parallax
Parallelfahrt, parallele Kamerafahrt – lateral dollyshot
Parallelschaltung – parallel connection, bypass
Parallelton-Verfahren – split sound system
Partner des Hauptdarstellers – co-star
Partner des Hauptdarstellers spielen – to act opposite the star
Passage – change-over
Passepartout – passepartout
Pausenzeichen – station identification signal, interval signal
Pegel – level
Pegelvordämpfung – attenuation
perfekte Filmkopie – moo print
Perforation – perforation
Perforationsloch – perforation hole, sprocket hole
Perforationslochabstand – perforation gauge
Perforationsseite – edge of perforation
perforierter Film – sprocketed film base
periskopischer Kameravorsatz – periscopic lens attachment
Perlleinwand – glass pearl screen, pearl screen
Person, die in einem Film mehrere Funktionen haben, z. B. Produzent, Regisseur und Schauspieler – hyphenate
Personal– staff
Perücke – periwig
Perückenmacher – wig-maker
Pfarrkino – parochial cinema

Pfeiffen – acoustical back coupling, acoustic feedback
Pflichtenheft – data sheet
phantomgespeistes Mikrofon – phantom powered microphone, simplex microphone
Phasenänderung – phase change, phase shift
Phasenbedingung – phase condition
Phasendifferenz – phase difference
Phasengang – phase response
phasengleich – in phase
Phasenlage – phase
Phasenregelung – phase control
Phasenschieber – field to frame synchronizer, phase shifter, video/film synchronizer
Phasenspannung – phase voltage
Phasenwinkel – phase angle
Phosphoreszenz – phosphorescence
Photometrie – photometry
Piezoelektrizität – piezoelectricity
Pilotfrequenz – pilot frequency
Pilotsignal – driving signal
Pilotton – pilot frequency
Pilottonverfahren – pilot frequency recording
Pinza – pincer, pup
Pinzalampe – clip lamp
Pistolengriff – pistolgrip
Planckscher Strahler – black body, full body
Planfilm – flat film, sheet film
Planfilmkassette – filmpack back, sheet film holder
plankonkav – plano-concave
Plankonvexlinse – plane-convex lens
Planspiegel – plane mirror
plastische Raumtonwirkung – stereo acoustics
Platine – circuit plate
Plattenspieler – turntable
Plattform für Schauspieler – apple box
Plattform mit halber Höhe – half-apple box
Polarisationsbrille – polarizing spectacles
Polarisationsfilter – pola screen

Polaroidmagazin – magazine for polaroid film
Polfilter – polarization filter
Positivbildmuster – picture dailies print
positive Amplitudenmodulation – **positive amplitude modulation**
positive Amplitudenmodulation – **positive amplitude modulation**
Positivfilm – print positive
Positivschwärzung – density of a positive
Potentiometer – potentiometer
Praktikabel – parallel (US), practicable, riser, rostrum (GB)
Praktikant – trainee
Prasseln – crackling
prasseln – to crackle
Presse – press
eine Presseerklärung abgeben – to make a statement of press
Presseagent – flack, press agent
Presseagentur – press agency
Presseausweis – press card
Pressebericht – press report, newspaper report
Pressechef – head of publicity, publicity manager
Presseempfang – press conference
Pressefreiheit – freedom of the press
Pressegesetz – press law
Pressekommentar – press commentary, press release
Pressekonferenz – press conference
Pressemeldung – press release
Pressestimmen – press review
Primärton – guidetrack
Primärvalenzen – primaries
Prinzipschema – skeleton diagram
Prisma – prism
Prismenfilter – prismatic lens, prism lens
Prismensucher – prism view-finder
Probeaufnahme – casting, rehearsal screen test, test take
Probedurchlauf – run-through, walk-through, dry run
Probe mit abgeschalteten Kameras – run-through
Produktion – production
Produktionsassistent – production assistant
Produktionsbericht – data sheet

Produktionschef – production manager
Produktionsetat – production budget
Produktionsfahrer – transportation
Produktionsfirma – production company
Produktionskompendium – production matte box
Produktionskosten – production costs
Produktionsleiter – associate producer, executive producer
Produktionsnummer – production number
Produktionsplan – production schedule, cross-plot
Produktionssekretärin – production secretary, production department secretary
Produktionsspiegel – chart of the pictures in production, chart of features in production
Produktionsversicherung – film producer's indemnity insurance
Produzent – producer
Programmangebot – program offer
Programmdirektor – director of programs
Programmwechsel – change of program
Projektion – projection
Projektionsbildwinkel – projection angle
Projektionsentfernung – projection distance
Projektionsfenster – projection gate
Projektionsobjektiv – projection lenses
Projektionsraumfenster – cabin window
Projektionswand – projection screen
Projektionswinkel – angle of projection, projection angle
Projektor – projection machine, projector
einen Projektor ausrichten – to align a projector
Projektorraum – booth
Prolongation – hold-over
prolongieren – to hold-over
Prompter – prompter
Propagandafilm – propaganda film
Prospekt (Hintergrund) – backdrop, background, backing
Prospektmaler – scenic artist
Prüfeinrichtung – test unit
Prüffeld – test department
Prüfspannung – testing voltage

Prüfungsausschuß – examining board
Pseudosolarisation – pseudosolarisation
Publikum – audience
Pulver, pulverförmig – powder
punktförmige Abbildung – point image
punktförmige Abtastung – direct scanning
punktgenaues fokussieren – hard focus
Pupille – pupil
Puppenfilm – puppet film
purpur – magenta
Pyrotechnik – pyrotechnics
Pyrotechniker – pyrotechnist

Q

quadrieren, eine Einstellung einrichten, den Bildausschnitt festlegen – to frame
Quarz – crystal
quarzgesteuert – crystal-controlled
Quarzmotor – crystal controlled motor, crystal motor
Quarzpilottonverfahren – cordless sync
Quecksilberdampflampe – mercury lamp
Quecksilberhochdrucklampe – high-pressure mercury lamp
Quelle – source
Querbild – horizontal image
Querschnitt – cross-section
Querschramme – transversal scratch
Querspurverfahren – transversal recording

R

Rahmenantenne – aerial frame
rahmen, Dias rahmen – to mount
Rahmenentwicklung – rack processing
Rahmensucher – frame view-finder
Rampenlicht – cyc-light, groundrow, limelight, striplight
randlos – marginless
Randnummer – edge number, key number
Randschärfe – definition on the border of the image, marginal definition, marginal sharpness
Randtonspur-Beschichtung durch Aufgiessen der Magnetschicht – magnetic striping
Rapidentwicklung – rapid developer
Raster – gauze, spun glass
Rasterabtastung – frame scanning
Rasterblende – masking plate
Rasterdeckung – image registration (US), picture superimposition (GB)
Rasterfilm – lenticulated film
Rasterstruktur – line structure
Raubkopie – pirated film
Rauchpfanne – smoke pot
Raumakustik – room acoustics
einen Raum akustisch abdämpfen – to damp a room
Raumatmo, Raumatmosphäre – room noise, room sound, room tone, wild sound
Raumbild – stereoscopic picture
Raumfilm – stereoscopic film
räumliches Fernsehen – stereoscopic television
Raumlicht – ambient light
Raumton – sound perspective
Raumwirkung des Bildes – plasticity
Rauschanteil – photo-electric noise level
Rauschen – noise
Rauschunterdrückung – noise reduction, noise elimination
Realisator – metteur-en-scene (*slang*)
Rechte – rights
Rechte an einer Kopie – rights per release print

rechte Bühnenseite – stage right
Rechtecksonnenblende – rectangular sunshade
Redakteur – editor
Redaktionsschluß – copy deadline, copy date
Reduzieradapter – step down ring, reducing adapter
Reflektor – reflector
Reflexionsfaktor – reflection factor
Reflexionswinkel – angle of reflection
Reflexsucher – reflex view-finder
Reflextionsverlust – reflection losses
Regelmotor, regelbarer Motor – variable-speed motor
Regelspannungssynchronisierung – phase synchronisation
Regenabweiser – panaclear
Regenerator – replenisher
regenerieren – to regenerate
Regenerierung eines Filmes – regeneration of film
Regenschutz – rain cover
Regie – direction
Regieanweisung – direction
Regieassistent – assistant director
Regiefenster – studio supervising window
Regie führen – to direct
Regiepult – control desk, master control board
Regieraum – master control room
Regiestab – stage direction
Regiestuhl – director's chair
Regionalfernsehen – local television
Regisseur – director
Regler – fader (unit)
reinigen – to clean
Reinigung der Tonbänder mit zwei Samttüchern – velveting sound
Reinigungsmittel – cleaning agent
Reisefilm – tourist film
Reisekosten – travel expenses
Reißschwenk – flash pan, swish pan, whip pan, zip pan
Reklame – publicity
Rekorderkamera – camcorder, combo, VTR in camera
Relais – relay
relative Öffnung – relative aperture

Reportage – topical film
Reportagefilm – report film
Reportagewagen – car for reportage and topicals, window unit
Reprise – reissue
Reproduktionszubehör – copying accessory
Requisite – extra, props
Requisiteur – property man, property master, set decorator
Resonanzkurve – resonance curve
Resonanzspitze – resonance peak
Restentladung – pre-discharge
Restladung – residual charge
Restlichtfotografie – available light photography
Restlichtkamera – low-light-level camera
Reststrom – leak current
Retouchiermesser – scraper
retuschieren – to retouch
Retuschierfarbe – retouching dye
Retuschierpinsel – retouching pencil
Revolverkopf – lens turret, turret head
Richtmikrofon, Kanone (*slang*) – directional microphone, shot gun, unidirectional microphone
Richtungseffekt – directional effect
Rohdrehbuch – treatment of the script, rough treatment
Rohfilm – raw stock
Rohfilmhersteller – raw stock manufacture
Rohfilmmaterial – raw stock (US), unexposed film
Röhre – tube
röhrenbestückt – tubed
Röhrenkennlinie – anode characteristic, dynamic characteristic, load time tube characteristic
Röhrenrauschen – tube hiss, tube noise, white noise, flat random noise
Rohrgitter – pipe grid
Rohschnitt – assembly, cutting copy, rough cut
Rollen besetzen – to cast
eine Rolle einstudieren – to get up a part, to coach an actor in a part
Rollenfach eines Schauspielers – line of an actor
Rollennummer – roll number
Rollfilm – roll film

Rollstativ – castered skid, rolling tripod, wheeled skid, wheeled tee, wheeled tie-down, wheeled triangle
Rolltitel – crawl title, rolling title
Rolltitelgerät – title drum
Romanbearbeitung – adaptation of a novel
Röntgenfotografie – X-ray photography
Röntgenkinematografie – X-ray cinematography
rot – red
roter Faden – running gag
Rotlicht – tally-light, tally
Rotlichtwarnlampe vor Studios – wigwag
Rückansicht – rear view
Rückbau – deconstruction
Rückblende – cut-back, flash-back
Rucken über H – bouncing (US)
Rückkopplung – acoustical back coupling, acoustic feedback
Rücklauf – reverse action
Rückleiter – return wire
Rückprojektion, Rückpro – back projection, back ground projection
Rückprojektionswand – transparent screen for rear projection
Rückschwingspiegel – instant return mirror
Rückspielverfahren – playback process
Rückteilwechselrahmen – interchangeable groundglass frame
Rufzeichen – callsign
Ruheschwärzung – unmodulated density
Ruhespur – unmodulated track
Ruhestrom – idle current
Rumpelgeräusch – rumble
Rundfunk – broadcast
Rundfunkgebühr – receiver licence fee
Rundfunksendung – audiobroadcasting
Rundfunksprecher – narrator
Rundfunkstörung – atmospherics, broadcast interference, BCI
Rundfunkstörung, die durch Störsender entsteht – jamming
Rundfunkstudio – broadcast studio
Rundhorizont – cylorama
Rundmagazin – rotary slide magazine
Runzelkorn – reticulation, wrinkling of gelatin
Rüstwagen – rigging tender

S

Sabattier-Effekt – pseudosolarisation
Sammellinse – collecting lens, converging lens, convex lens
Sättigung – saturation
Satzobjektiv – combination set of lenses
Satz von Objektiven – lens set
Schabemesser – scraper
Schablonenlichtblende – cookie (*slang*)
Schachbrettestbild – checkerboard pattern, chessboard pattern
Schalenentwicklung – dish development
Schallblende – sound gobo
schalldicht – sound proof
Schalleistung – acoustical output, acoustical power
Schallfeld – acoustical field
Schallplattenverstärker – gramophone amplifier
Schallquelle – acoustical source
Schallschutzgehäuse – blimp
Schallschutzhaube – barney
Schallschutzwand – baffle
schalltot – acoustically dead
schalltoter Raum – dead room, anechoic room
Schallwand – baffle
Schaltbild – circuit diagram
Schalter – switch
Schaltfrequenz – sampling frequency
Schaltkontakt – switch contact
Schaltplan – circuit diagram, switching schedule
Schalttafel – distribution board
Schaltuhr – adjustable timer, timer
Schärfe – acuity, focus, sharpness
Schärfeassistent – focus operator, focus puller
Schärfe des Bildes – definition of the picture
Schärfemarkierung – focus mark
Schärfentiefe – depth-of-field
die Schärfe auf einen Punkt legen, um andere Bildteile in der Unschärfe zu halten – differential focusing
die Schärfe nachziehen – to rack focus, to throw focus

die Schärfe ziehen – to focus, to pull focus, to ride focus, to throw focus
Schärfentiefenskala – depth-of-field scale
Schärfenverlagerung – split-focus shot
Schärfenziehhebel – focus lever
Schärfenziehvorrichtung – follow focus mechanism
scharfstellen – to focus
Schatten – shadow
Schattendurchzeichnung – shadow detail
Schattierung – shade
Schaum – foam
Schauplatz der Handlung – locale, locality, scene of action
Schauspieler – actor
Schauspieler engagieren – to cast
Schauspielerin – actress
Schauspielnachwuchs – young artists
Schauspieltruppe – cast, crew
Scheimpflug' sche Verschwenkung – Scheimpflug adjustment
Scheinwerfer – reflector, studio lights
Scheinwerferführung – reflector direction
Scheinwerfermaske, um Schatten zu erzeugen – cookie, cucaloris
Scheunentor (*slang*) – barndoor
Schicht – coating
Schichtband – coating tape
Schichtseite – emulsion side, side of coating
Schiene – rails
Schienenrad – truck wheel
Schirmgitter – screen grid
Schirmgitterspannung – screen voltage
Schlagschatten – heavy shadow, cast shadow, hard shadow
Schleichwerbung – incidental advertising, plug, product placement
Schleier – fog, veiling
Schleife loop
Schleifenprojektor – loop projector
Schleifenschutz – loop protector
Schliere – cloudy streams, streak
Schlierenkinematografie – cinematography of medium with variable optical densities
Schlitzblende – slit diaphragm

Schlitzverschluß – focal plane shutter
Schlußeinstellung – closing scene
Schlußklappe – endboard
Schlußszene – closing scene
Schmalfilm – substandard film
Schmalfilm (16mm) – narrow gauge film
Schmalfilmformat – substandard film size
Schmalfilmkamera – substandard film camera
Schmalfilmprojektor – substandard film projector
Schmalfilmverleih – substandard film distribution
Schminke – grease-paint, make-up, paint
schminken – to make-up
Schminkmeister – make-up supervisor
Schminktisch – make-up table
Schnappschuß – grap-shot, snapshot
Schnappschußeinstellung – zone focusing
Schneckengetriebe – worm drive, worm gear
schneiden – to edit
Schneideraum – cutting room, editing room, edit suite
Schneideraummiete – cutting room rental
Schneidetisch – cutting bench, editing table
schneller Rücklauf – quick reverse, quick reverse action
schneller Vorlauf – quick forward action
Schnellfixierbad – rapid fixer
Schnellschaltwerk – fast pulldown recorder
Schnelltransportkurbel – rapid-winding crank
Schnellwechselkassette – quick change magazine
Schnitt – cut
»Schnitt!« (Ende einer Szene), Anweisung des Regisseurs – »Cut!«
Schnittbildentfernungsmesser – split-image range-finder
Schnittbilder – bridge, cutaways, cut-in, pick-up, sectional view
Schnittfolge – cutting order
Schnittkopie – cutting copy, work print
Schnittliste – editing list, continuity list, cutting-room log, logbook
Schnittmaterial – tape for editing, uncut tape, trims, offcuts
Schnittmeister für die Musik – music editor
Schnittpunkt – cutting point
Schnittreste – out-takes

Schnittsteuerung – edit controller
Schnittstudio – edit suite (GB)
Schnittweite – distance between lens vertex and back focus, width of cut
Schrägaufnahme – oblique shot
schräge Klebestelle – diagonal splice
schräge Schnittstelle – diagonal cut
schräge Tonklebestelle – oblique sound film splice
Schrägprojektion – oblique projection
Schramme – scar, scratch, shadow scratch
Schrammen und Kratzer, die durch Filmsalat verursacht werden – abraisions
Schriftgeber, Schriftgenerator – character generator, compositer
Schrumpfung – shrinkage
Schrumpfung des Filmmaterials – shrinkage of the film
Schulfunk – school radio, school broadcasting
Schulterstativ – shoulder pod
Schulterstütze – body brace
schütteln – to agitate
Schutzbeschichtung – preservative
Schutzerde – protective earth, protective ground, non-fused earth
Schutzgeländer – hand rail
Schutzschicht – protecting coat
Schwalbenschwanz – dovetail
schwarzer Körper – black body, full body
Schwarzfilm, Schwarzfilmvorspann – black leader
Schwarzpegel – black level, pedestal, Y-level, picture black
Schwarzsignal – dark spot signal
Schwärzung – density
Schwärzungskurve – characteristic curve
schwarzweiß – black-and-white
Schwarzweißfernseher – mono set (US)
Schwarzweißfilm – black-and-white film
Schwarzweißkamera – monochrome camera
Schwarzweißmonitor – monochrome monitor
Schwarzwert – black level, pedestal, Y-level, picture black
Schwarzwertanhebung – black stretch
Schwarzwertbegrenzung – black clipping
Schwarzwertklemmung – black-level clamping

Schwebungsfrequenz – beat frequency
Schwenk – pan shot
Schwenkarm – panhandle, panning handle
schwenkbarer Sucher – pivoting view-finder, tiltable view-finder
schwenken (horizontal) – to pan
schwenken (vertikal) – to tilt
Schwenker – cameraman, camera operator
Schwenkgriff – grip
Schwenkstativ – cradle head
Schwingung – oscillation
Schwungmasse, Schwungrad – balance wheel, flywheel
Scriptgirl – continuity girl, script girl
Sehbeteiligung – viewing figure
sehr große Einstellung – big close up, BCU
sehr kurzer Zwischenschnitt – flash
Sehschärfe – visual acuteness (US)
Sehvermögen – vision
Seidenblende – silk
Seitenbeleuchtung – side lighting
Seitenlicht – cross light, edge light, side light
Seitenschneider – side-cutting plier
Seitenumkehr – lateral inversion
seitenverkehrte Abbildung – laterally inverted image
Seitenverschiebung – horizontal shift
seitliche Dollyfahrt – crabbing, tracking shot
seitliche Kamerafahrt – crabbing
Sekundärwicklung – secondary coil
Selbstauslöser – auto timer, self timer
selbstfahrender Kran – cherry picker
Selbstregelmotor – constant speed motor, servo motor
selbstregelnder Verstärker – automatic gain control
selbsttätige Helligkeitsregelung – automatic brightness control
selbsttätige Synchronisationsschaltung – automatic locking circuit
selbsttätige Weißwertbegrenzung – automatic peak limiting
Selenzelle – selenium cell
Sendeanstalt – broadcasting house
Sendeband – channel
Sendefolge – run-down

Sendegebiet – coverage, service area, range of reception
Sendeleistung – transmitting power
Sendeleiter – production manager, production director
senden – to air, to be on the air, to take the air
Sendenorm – transmission standard
Sender – transmitter
Senderkette – transmission chain
Senderreichweite – radius of the service area
Sendeschluß – close of transmission, close-down
Sendeturm – transmission tower
Sendezeit – time of transmission, broadcasting time, transmission time, air time, slot, spot
die Sendezeit überziehen – to overrun
Sendezentrale – master control room
Sendung – transmission
Senkelband – 1/4 inch tape
Senkrechtaufnahme – perpendicular view
senkrechte Bildlageschwankung – bouncing, jumping
Sensibilisierung – sensitizing
Sensitometer – sensitometer
Sensitometrie – sensitometry
Serienkopie – release print
Servo-Hochlaufzeit – servo-lock time
Sicherheitseinstellung – insurance take
Sicherheitsfilm – safebase film, safety film
Sicherheitsvorschriften – anti-firing regulations, security ~
Sicherung – fuse
Sichtbarmachung – visualization
Sichtgerät – monitor, display
sich verhaspeln – to get muddled, to fluff
Signalausfall – drop-out
Signalgröße – signal level
Signalleuchte an der Fernsehkamera. – tally light
Signaluhr – signalling clock
Signalverzerrung – signal distortion
Silben verschlucken – to slur, to swallow
Silberblende – reflector
Silberrückgewinnung – recuperation of the silver, silver recovery

Skala – dial
Soffite – tubular light
Sofortbildfilm – instant print film
Softscheibe – scrim
Sollfrequenz, Sollgeschwindigkeit – nominal frequency
Sonnenblende – lens hood, sunshade
Sonnenstrahlung – solar radiation
Spalt – gap
Spannung – voltage
Spannungsstabilisierung – voltage stabilization
Spannungsverstärkung – voltage amplification
Spannungswähler – voltage adapter
Spätvorstellung – night performance
Speicherplattenschicht – target layer
Speicherröhre – charge-storage tube
Speisemodul – powering unit
Speisespannung – supply voltage
Speisung – power supply, charge, feeding, energize
Spektrum – spectrum
Sperrgepäck – bulky baggage
Sperrgreifer – pilot pins, register pin, registration pin
Sperrschicht – barrier layer, blocking layer, insulating layer
Sperrschichtzelle – photocell blocking layer
Sperrspannung – blocking bias, reverse voltage, inverse voltage
Spesen – per diem
Spesenabrechnung – account of expenses
Spezial-Effekte – special effects
Spezial HMI-Lampe (25kW), die bei einer amerikanischen Nacht Mondlicht simuliert – flying moon
sphärische Aberration – spherical aberration
Spiegel – mirror
Spiegel für den Parallaxenausgleich – anti-parallax mirror
Spiegelkugel – mirror ball
Spiegellampe – mirror lamp
Spiegelreflexkamera – reflex camera
Spielfilm – feature
eine Spielfilmszene durch Statisten beleben – to animate a dead scene
Spielplan – schedule of features

Spielzeit eines Films – running time
Spingblende – automatic diaphragm, semi-automatic diaphragm
Spinnwebmaschine – cobweb gun
spiralförmige Blende – spiral fade, spiral dissolve
Spiralkabel – coil-cord, helix cable
Spiralstromkabel – coiled power cord
Spitze – hair light
eine Spitze setzen – to set a hair light
Spitzenwert – maximum rating, peak value
Spitzenwertmesser – peak indicator
Spitze, Spitzlicht – hair light, kick-light, rim-light
Sponsorsendung – sponsored broadcast
Sportkommentator – sport commentator
Sportschau – television (TV) sports news
Sportsendung – sports news programs, sports and events
Sportsucher – sports view-finder
Spotmeter – spot photometer
Sprachaufnahme – dialogue recording, recording of the commentary
Sprachband – speech band
Sprachszene – dialogue scene
Spratzer – sputter, splash
Sprecher – speaker
Sprecherkabine – commentator's booth
Sprecherplatz – commentator's position
Sprecherraum – announcer studio
Sprecherstudio – continuity studio
Sprecher über einer fremdländischen Fassung, die im Hintergrund hörbar bleibt – voice over
Sprechfunkgerät – walkie-talkie
Sprech-Hörkopf – combined recording reproducing head
Sprechkopf – recording head
Sprechtitel – spoken title
Spritzfleck – splash
Sprossenschrift bei Lichtton – variable density recording
Sprungwand – camera trap, wild wall (*slang*)
Spulenkern – core of the bobbin
Spulentonbandgerät – reel-to-reel recorder
Spule, Spulenarm – reel

Spurhaltung – tape guidance, tracking
Spurlage – track placement, track position
Stabilisierbad – stabilizer
Stabliste – production list
Stahlbajonettfassung – steel bayonet mount
Stammlösung – stock solution
Standbild – freeze frame, freeze
Standbildfotograf – stills photographer
Standbildkamera – still camera
Standbildprojektion – still projection
Standbildverlängerung – freeze frame, hold frame, stop frame
Standfoto – still photograph
Standpunkt – point of view
Stanze für Gelatinefilterfolien – cutter for gelatin foil, filter foil pouch
Stanztisch – notching table
Starkstrom – heavy current, large current
Startband – film leader, leader, sync leader, tape leader
Starterlösung – starting solution, starter
Startmarkierung – startmarking
Startvorlaufzeit – preroll time
Statist – crowd artist
Stativ – legs (*slang*), stand, tripod, grip stand
Stativbein – tripod leg
Stativfuteral – tripod case
Stativgewinde – tripod turn
Stativkopf – pan-and-tilt head, tripod head
Stativmutter – bush
Stativschnellkupplung – tripod quick-coupling
Stativspinne – crowsfoot, spider, stand, tee, triangle
Stativverlängerung – tripod lengthening
Staubablagerung – deposit of dust
Staubkorn – dust particle
Staubschutz – dust cover
Steckdose – outlet, socket
Stecker – plug
Steckfeld – patch bay, patchboard, patch panel
Steckleiste – spider box
Steiger, selbstfahrender Kran – cherry picker

steile Gradation – steep graduation
Steilheit – gamma
Stereoakustik – stereo acoustics
Stereofilm – stereoscopic film
Stereofonie – stereophony
stereofonisch – stereophonic
Stereomischpult – stereo-mixer
Stereoprojektion – stereoscopic projection
Stereoskopie – stereoscopy
Stereoton – stereophonic sound
Steuerring – control ring
Steuerspur – control track, cue track
Stimmung – mood
Stopbad – stop bath
Stopfixierbad – stop fixer
Stoptrick – freeze effect
Störabstand – S/N ratio
Störgeräusch – leaking noise
Störpegel – parasitic noise level
Störsender – jamming transmitter
Störung des Hilfsträgers – subcarrier beat
stottern – to fluff
Strahlablenkung – beam deflection
Strahlaustastung beim Zeilenrücklauf – beam suppression, blanking during flyback
Strahlenteiler – beam splitter
Strahlschärfe – beam focus
Strahlstrom – beam current
Strahlung – radiation
Strahlunterdrückung – beam gate
Streulicht – stray light
Streulichtschirm – diffusing screen
Streuung – aberration, variation
Streuwinkel – stray angle
Strippe (*slang*) – line
Strom – current
Stromaggregat – generating set
Stromänderung – alteration of current

Stromgenerator – jenny (*slang*)
Stromkreis – circuit
Stromstärke – amperage, intensity of current
Stromversorgung – power supply
Stromverteiler, Mehrfachsteckdose – spider box
Studioarbeiter – grip
Studioaufbau – studio setting
Studioausgangsbild – outgoing signal
Studioaußengelände – back lot, lot
Studiodekor, Studiodekoration – abstract set (US), studio decoration (GB)
Studiodirektor – studio manager
Studiodisposition – studio allocation-schedule, studio bookings
Studiokamera – studio camera, view camera
Studiomiete – studio rent
Studioredakteur – presenting editor, anchor man
Studioregisseur – studio director
Studioscheinwerfer – studio lighting
Studiotechnik – studio engineering
Studiovorarbeiter – key grip
Stufenkeil – grey scale, photometric steptype wedge
Stufenlinsenscheinwerfer – florentine, Fresnel lens spotlight, plano-convex spot, PC spot
stumme Einstellung – wild picture
stumme Filmkopie – action track, mute (GB)
Stummfilm – silent movie
Stumpfklebepresse, Stumpfklebelade – butt joiner, butt splice
stürzende Linie – converging line toward the top of the image, converging vertical
subjektive Kamera, Substitution – point-of-view shot, subjective camera treatment
substraktives Farbverfahren – substractive color system
subtraktive Farben – substractive color
Sucher – finder, view-finder
Sucherbild – picture area
Sucherkasch – view-finder frame
Sucherlupe – view-finder magnifier, magnifier
Sucherlupenhalterung – eyepiece leveler
Sucherlupenverlängerung – extension view-finder, finder extender

Sucher mit automatischer Bildaufrichtung – orientable view-finder
Sucherobjektiv – view-finder lens, viewing lens
Sucherokular – view-finder eyepiece
Summenregler – group fader (*slang*)
Summensignal – composite signal
Superikonoskop – super iconoscope
symetrischer Mikrofoneingang – balanced microphone input
synchroner Antrieb – synchronous drive
Synchrongeschwindigkeit (24, 25 oder 30 B/s) – silent speed
Synchronisation – locking
Synchronisation aus einer Fremdsprache in die eigene Sprache – dubbing
Synchronisation einer fremdsprachigen Version – foreign language operation
Synchronisierungsbereich – hold range
Synchronität – syncing
Synchronklappe – camera marker, clapp stick, clapper, clapper board, scene slate, slate
Synchronmarke – synchronizing mark, sync mark, sync pop
Synchronmarke durch Klappe – clapper mark
Synchronmotor – interlock motor, synchronous motor
Synchronpunkt – sync point
Synchronschleife – dubbing loop, post-sync loop
Synchronsprecher – dubbing speaker, dubbing actor
Synchronstudio – dubbing theatre
Synchronumroller – synchronizer, synchronous winder
Synchronzeichen – synchronizing mark
Szene – scene
eine Szene durchspielen – to run through a scene
eine Szene einrichten – to set up a shot
Szenenauflösung – coverage
Szenenbild – set, setting, decor, scenery
Szenenumbau – to re-dress
Szenenwechsel – change of scene

T

Tageskommentar – daily commentary
Tageslicht – daylight
Tageslichtkassette – daylight magazine
Tageslichtleuchtstoffröhre – daylight-type fluorescent tube
Tageslichtprojektor – overhead projector
Tageslichtspule – daylight loading spool
tägliche Aufführung – daily performance
Takt – clock
Taktgeber – sync generator, sync signal generator
Talentsucher – talent scout
Tankentwicklung – tank development
Tastatur – keyboard
Tauchspulmikrofon – moving coil microphone
1000Hz-Ton aufschalten – to put on 1.000Hz
1000W Scheinwerfer – ashan
1000W Strahler – can
1000W Stufenlinsenscheinwerfer – ace
T-Blendenwert – T-stop
Team – crew, team, unit
Teamwagen – camera car
Technicolorverfahren – three-strip
technischer Berater – technical adviser
Teilbelichtung – partial exposure
Teilmaske – partial mask
telegen – telegenic
Telekonverter – extender, range extender, tele-converter
Teleobjektiv – telephoto lens
Teleprompter – auto cue, prompter
Temperatur – temperature
Temperaturausgleich – compensation of temperature
terminieren – to bill
Terminplan – schedule
Testband zur Einstellung der Spaltöffnung beim Magnetkopf – azimuthal alignment tape
Testbild – test pattern

Testbild für die Gammakorrektur – cross-gamma pattern
Testsignal für Schwarz – artificial black signal
Testsignal für Weiß – artificial white signal
Teststreifen – control strip
Texter – ad writer, script-writer, scripter
Textgeber, Textprojektor – auto-cue, prompter
Text zu einem Bild – caption
Theaterakustik – auditorium acoustics
Theaterkopie – release print, show print
Tiefenabsenkung – bass cut filtering
Tiefenanhebung – bass boost
Tiefenfilter – bass cut filter
tiefen gelöschtes Band – clean tape
Tiefenschärfe – depth-of-field, depth-of-focus, shallow depth, shallow focus
Tiefenschärfeanzeige – depth-of-field indicator
Tiefenschärfebereich – zone of sharpness
Tiefenschärfetabelle – depth-of-field table
tiefer Ton – low sound
Tiefpaß – low-pass filter
Tieftonlautsprecher – woofer
Tieftonsystem – bass system
Timecodeleser – time-code reader
Titel – credits, credit title, main title, production credits, title
Titelaufnahme – title photographing
Titelgerät – movie titler
Titelinsert – caption
Titelkarton – art board, fashion board
Titelkasch – safe title area
Titelmusik – opening music
Titelnegativ – title negative
Titelständer – caption stand
Titeluntergrund – title background
Titelvorlage – title card, title cartoon
Titelvorspann mit den Namen des technischen Stabes – technical credits
Ton – sound
Ton/Bildversatz – advance
»Ton ab!« Anweisung an den Tonmeister – »Roll sound!«
Tonabblende – sound fade

Tonabnehmer – pick-up
Tonabteilung – sound department
tonadergespeistes Mikrofon – A-B powered microphone, T-powered microphone
Tonangel – fishing rod, fishpole, mike boom
Tonangler – boom operator
Ton anlegen – synchronizing rushes
Ton-Arbeitskopie – scratch track
Tonarchiv – record office, sound library, tape library
Tonaufnahme – record
Tonaufnahmegerät – sound system
Tonaufnahme ohne Bild – wildtrack
Tonaufnahmewagen – mobile recording unit
Tonaufzeichung (Vorgang) – sound recording
Tonaufzeichnungsverfahren – sound recording system
Tonausrüstung – sound equipment
Ton aussteuern – to dial, to pot
Tonband – sound tape, tape
Tonbandgerät – tape machine
Tonbandgerät mit drei Tonspuren – triple-track recorder
Tonbandmaterial – magnetic recording medium
Tonbericht – sound report, sound reports sheet
Tonbildschau – sound-slide show
Tonblubbern – bloop
Toncutter/in – sound editor
Toneingang – channel
Tonempfindung – acoustical perception
Tonfilm – talking film, sound film
Tonfilmprojektor – sound projector
Tonfilmstudio – sound stage
Tonfrequenz – pitch
Tonfrequenzen oberhalb von 20 kHz – superaudible frequency
Tonhöhe – peak of sound, pitch, pitch of sound, tone pitch
Tonhöhenregler – tone control
Tonhöhenschwankungen – pitch variation, wow and flutter
Tonhöhenschwankungen durch unregelmäßigen Bandlauf – wow and flutter
Toningenieur – sound engineer

Tonkanal – audiofrequency channel, sound channel
Tonklebestelle – sound film splice
Tonknacker – clapper mark
Tonkopf – audio head, sound head
Tonkopiermaschine – sound printer
Tonlampe – sound exiter lamp
Tonlampengleichrichter – exciter lamp rectifier
»Ton läuft!«, Antwort auf »Ton ab!« – »Tape is on speed!«
Tonlaufwerk – sound head
Tonmann – knob twister (*slang*), mixer, recordist, sound man, technical operator
Tonmeister – chief recorder
Tonmeister für die Mischung – mixer
Tonmischpult – audiomixer, sound mixer
Tonmischung – re-recording
Tonnegativ – sound negative, sound track negative
tonnenförmige Verzeichnung – barrel distortion
Tonpegel – sound level, volume
Tonpositiv – sound positive
Tonprobe – sound level check, sound test
Tonqualität – quality of sound, quality of tone
Tonregieraum – sound apparatus room
Tonregler – sound fader
Tonschleife – sound loop
Tonschnitt – sound editing
Tonsignal – audio signal, aural signal, sound signal
Tonspur – sound track
Tonspurlage – sound track placement
Tonstartmarkierung – sound start mark
Tonstudio – mixing room, sound recording studio
Tontechnik – acoustic engineering, sound technics
Tontechniker – sound mixer, sound operator
Tonträger – sound carrier
Tonüberblendung – cross fade, cross dissolve, seque, sound change-over, sound mixing, sound fading
Tonwertrichtigkeit von Farben – accuracy of color value
Tonwiedergabe – acoustical reproduction, sound reproduction
Tonzwischenfrequenz – sound intermediate frequency

Tonzwischenträgersystem – inter carrier sound system
Topf mit Kunsteis, um Nebel zu erzeugen – rumble pot
Torblende – barndoor
Totale – distance shot, long shot, total view, vista shot
Träger – carrier
Träger bei Film- und Videobändern – base
Trägerfrequenz – carrier frequency, picture tone
Trageriemen – carrying strap, shoulder strap
Tragetasche – transport case
Trailer – trailer
Transfokator – variofocal lens, transfocator, zoom-lens
Transparenz – transparency
Transportgreifer – feeding claws, pull down claw
Transversalverfahren – variable area sound recording system
Trapezverzeichnung – key stone
Treatment – draft script, treatment
Trennschärfe – adjacent channel selectivity
Tribüne – rostrum
Trick – special trick
Trickarbeit – trick work
Trickaufnahme – trick shot
Trickaufnahme durch eine Glasscheibe, auf die fehlende Teile des Hintergrundes gemalt sind – glass shot
Trickaufnahme mit Glasscheibe – Pepper's ghost set-up
Trickblende – wipe, optical
Trickfilm – animated cartoon
Trickfilmfigur – cartoon, toon (*slang*)
Trickfilmkamera – cartoon camera
Trickfilmphase – cell, phase
Trickfilmzeichner – animator
Trickkamera – animated screen camera, bench camera, rostrum camera
Trickmischer – special effects generator, animation mixer
Tricktaste – trick button, animation camera trigger
Tricktisch – rostrum bench, cartoon camera bench, animation stand, stop-frame rostrum, trick table
Tricktitel – animated caption
Tricküberblendung – animation superimposition
Trittschall – impact sound

Trittschallfilter – impact-sound filter
trocken – dry
Trockenbatterie – dry cell
Trockenfleck – drying mark
Trockenklebefolie – dry-mounting tissue
Trockenschrank – drying box
Tüll – diffusor (screen), gauze, tulle
Tute für Scheinwerfer – snoot
TV-Gerät – television reciever, TV set

U

überarbeiten (einen Text) – to re-write
überarbeitete Fassung – revised draft
Überarbeitung – re-write
überbelichten – to overexpose
überbelichteter Film – bleached out film
Überbelichtung – over-exposure
überblenden – to fade, to superimpose
Überblendung – dissolve
Überblendung durch Unschärfe – defocus mix
Überblendung zweier Reißschwenks – swish dissolve
Überblendzeichen – change-over cue, change-over mark, change-over signal, cue dot
über den Sender gehen – to air, to be on the air, to take the air
über den Sender gehen – to air, to be on the air, to take the air
überentwickeltes Negativ – overdevelopded negative
Überentwicklung – over developing
Übergabepunkt an Fernsehleitungen – video interconnection point
überhängen – to hang over
überlagern – to superimpose
überlagertes Bild – superimposed image
Überlänge – overlength
Überleitungsszene – transitional scene
Überleitung von einer Szene zur anderen – segue
Überprüfen des Signals mit Messgeräten – to ride the gain, to ride the spot, to ride the needle
überschreiben – to overseam
Überschrift – caption
Überschwinger – overshoot
Übersicht – general view, survey
Übersichtsaufnahme – total view, vista shot
Übersichtseinstellung – cover shot
Überspannung – overvoltage
überspielen – to transcribe, to transfer
Überspielung – re-recording, transfer, video-tape dubbing
Übersprechen (durchkopieren) von gewickeltem Magnetfilm – print-through

Übersteuerung – overmodulation
Übersteuerung (zu laut) – blasting
Überstrahlung – bloom, blooming, flare
Überstrahlung auf dem Film – hot spot
Übertragungsnorm – transmission standard
Überziehen – to spread
UKW Empfänger – short-wave reciever
ultraviolet – ultraviolet
ultraviolet durchlässig – transparent to ultraviolet
ultraweich – ultra soft
Umfahrt – developing shot
Umformer – converter
Umkehrbelichtung – reversal exposure
Umkehrentwicklung – developing reversal
Umkehrfilm – positive print, reversal film
Umkehrprisma – image erecting prism
Umkehrverfahren – reversal process
Umlaufblende – rotary shutter
Umlenkgetriebe – angular geared base
Umlenkprisma – deviation prism
Umriß – outline
umrollen – to respool, to rewind
Umroller – film winder, rewinder
Umrolltisch – winding bench
umschneiden – to cut, to re-edit
Umschnitt – edit down
Umsetzer – fill-in transmitter
Umsetzung in Bilder – visualization
umspielen – to re-record
umspulen – to respool
unbeabsichtigter Ton-Bild Versatz – slippage of sound to picture
unbelichteter Filmrest – short end
unbelichtetes Filmmaterial – raw stock (US), unexposed film
unbunt – achromatic, achromatically
Unbuntbereich – achromatic locus
Unendlicheinstellung – focused at infinity, infinity focusing, infinity focus
ungeblimbte Filmkamera – wild camera
ungekürzt – unabridged

universal Objektivstütze – universal lens support
Universal-Schärfenziehvorrichtung – universal follow focus mechanism
Universaltasche – compartment case
Universalvergrößerer – universal larger
unscharf – blurred, hazy, without contrast
Unschärfe – blurring, breezing, fringing
Unschärfe als künstlerischer Effekt – soft focus
Unschärfenblende – defocus mix
unscharfes Bild – fuzzy (*slang*), unsharp image
unsymetrischer Mikrofoneingang – unbalanced microphone input
Unterbelichtung – under-exposure
Unterbrechungsbad – stop bath
unterdrehen – to shoot with low speed, to undercrank
unterdrehte Aufnahme – quick motion, stop motion, time accelerator, time-lapse, undercrank
untere Filmschleife – bottom loop
Unterentwicklung – underdevelop
Unterlänge – underfootage
untermalende Musik – background music
Unterricht mit audio-visuellen Medien – audiovisual education
Unterrichtsfilm – teaching film
Unterspannung – undervoltage
Untertitel – burn-in, subtitle, caption
untertiteln – to subtitle
untertitelte Filmkopie – superimposed print
Unterwassergehäuse – underwater blimp, underwater housing
Unterwasserkamera – submarine camera, underwatercamera
unverkoppelt – free-running
Uraufführung – premier, first night, first run
Urheber – author, originator
Urheberrecht – author's rights, copyright
UV-Sperrfilter – haze filter
Ü-Wagen – car for reportage and topicals, minicam van, OB vehicle, OB van, radio OB

V

variable Sektorenblende – shutter control
Varioobjektiv – variable focus lens, zoom lens
Vektorskop – vectorscope
verarbeiten – to process
verbinden – to connect
Verbindungskabel – connection cable
verbleiben – to remain
Verbrauchsmaterial – production consumables
verdichten, die Brennweite verlängern – zoom-in shot
verdunkeln – to dim
verdünnen – to dilute
Verdünnung – dilution
veredeln – to texture
Verfasser – writer
verfilmen – to screen
Verfilmungsrecht – screen rights
Verfolgerlicht – follow spotlight
Verfolgungsaufnahme – follow shot
Verfolgungsscheinwerfer – follower, follow-spot, super trooper
vergilben – to turn yellow
Vergilbung – yellow discoloration, yellowing
Vergleichsbild – reference pattern
Vergleichstest – comparison test
Vergnügungssteuer – admission tax, entertainment tax
Vergrößerer – enlarger
vergrößern – to enlarge
Vergrößerung – blow-up
Vergrößerung eines Filmbilds – action still
Vergrößerungsmaßstab – magnification, scale of reproduction
vergütetes Objektiv – bloomed lens
Vergütung – antireflex layer of a lens
Verhältnis – ratio
verkitten – to cement
Verkleinerung – reduction
Verkleinerungskopie – reduction print

Verkopplung – locking
Verkopplungszeit – servo-lock time
verkratzter Film – rain of a film
Verlängerungsfaktor – filter factor, multiplication factor, prolongation factor
Verlängerungskabel – extension cord
Verlauffilter – gradual filter, graduated filter
Verleiher – distributer
Verleihfirma – distribution company
Verleihkopie – release print, show print
Verleihvertrag – distribution contract
Verlesen der Nachrichten, sobald sie aus dem Telex kommen – to rip and read
Verminderung der Farbsättigung – desaturation
verringern – to decrease
Versandabteilung – shipping department
Verschluß – shutter
Verschlußhebel – lockdown knob
den Verschluß spannen – to close the shutter
Verschlußzeit – shutter time
Verschnitt – waste
verschobener Bildstrich beim Filmprojektor – out of rack
Verschwenkung nach Scheimpflug – Scheimpflug adjustment
versprechen – to fluff
Versprecher – fluff
verstärken – to amplify
Verstärkerausgangsspannung – amplifier output voltage
Verstärkung – amplification, gain
Verstärkungsfaktor – amplifying factor
Verstärkungsstufe – stage of amplification
verstellbare Sektorenblende – variable shutter
Verstellplatte – camera slide
Verstellweg – adjustment facility
Versuchssendung – pilot program
Verteilerdose – spider box
Vertikalaustastimpuls – blanking pulse
Vertikalimpuls – field impulse, field synchronizing impulse, field sync signal, frame impulse, frame synchronizing impulse, frame sync signal

vertikal schwenken – to tilt
vertonen – to add sound to a film
Vervielfältigungsrechte von Filmen – film rights
Verwertungsvertrag – distribution contract
Verzerrung – distortion
verzerrungsfrei – distortionless
Verzögerungsglied – delay
Videoabgleich – video alignment
Videoaufzeichnung – video recording
Videoausgangssignal – video output
Videoband für den 1-Zoll B-Standard (C-Standard) – video tape Type B (video tape Type C)
Videobildgleichrichter – video detector
Videoendstufe – video final stage
Videofrequenz – video frequency
Videokabel – video cable
Videokassettenrekorder – video cartridge recorder, video cassette recorder
Videokopf – video head
Videokopfrad – video head wheel
Videomeßdienst – video quality control
Videonachbearbeitung (Schnitt, Mischung, Sprachaufnahme) – post production
Videoprüfsignalgeber – video test signal generator
Videorekorder – video tape recorder
Videoschaltpult – vision mixer panel
Videoschnitt und Nachbearbeitung – post production
Videosignal – video signal, picture signal
Videosignal durchschleifen – to loop the video signal
Videospur – video track
Videotechniker – video tape operator
Videothek – video-tape library
Videoträgerwelle – video carrier
Videoumschalter – video switch
Videoverkopplung – video locking
Videoverteiler – video distributor, video matrix
Vidikon – vidicon
Vielfachinstrument – multi-range measuring instrument
Vielfachstecker – spider box

4-Ebenenbildmischer – A-B-C-D cut mixer
Viertelspur – quarter track
1/4 Zoll Tonband – 1/4 inch tape
Vignette – cash, matte, vignette
V-Impuls – field impulse, field synchronizing impulse, field sync signal, frame impulse, frame synchronizing impulse, frame sync signal
violett – violet
virtuelles Bild – aerial image, virtual image
Vision – vision
Vogelperspektive – bird's eye view, high-angle shot, high-photography, high-shot
Vollausschlag auf der Skala – full-scale deflection
Vollaussteuerung – full modulation
Vollbild des Fernsehens – two-field picture
Vollpegel – fullmodulation, maximum level
Vollspur – full track
Volontär – trainee
von links nach rechts – left-to-right
von links nach rechts – left-to-right
von rechts nach links – richt-to-left
von rechts nach links – richt-to-left
Vorbaubühne – pre-assembly shop
vorbauen – to pre-assemble
Vorbauhalle – pre-assembly studio, pre-setting studio
Vorbeifahrt – run-by
Vorberuhigungsrolle – breaked idler roller
Vorbesichtigung – location survey
Vorderansicht – front view
Vorderblende – anterior shutter
vorderer Objektivdeckel – front lens cap
vordere Standarte – front standard
Vordergrund – foreground
Voreinstellung – preset
Vorfilm – supplementary film
vorführen – to project
Vorführer – projectionist
Vorführgenehmigung – projection permit
Vorführkabine – projection booth

Vorführraum – viewing theatre, screening room
Vorführrechte – exhibition rights
Vorführung – projection
Vorhang – curtain
Vorhärtebad – prehardener
Vorhören – apre-for listening
Vorlauf – forward action
vorläufiger Titel – provisional title, working title
vorletzte Einstellung eines Drehtags – Abby singer shot
Vormagnetisierung – magnetic biasing, pre-magnetising
vormischen – to pre-mix
Vormischung – pre-mix, pre-mixing
Vor- oder Nachspann – production credits
Vorprogramm – prologue
Vorratslösung – stock solution
Vorsatzlinse – additional lens, front lens, supplementary lens
Vorschaltgerät für HMI-Leuchten – ballast
Vorschaubild – monitor picture
Vorschaumonitor – preview monitor
Vorschulprogramm – pre-school broadcasting
Vorspannband – leader tape
Vorspannfilm – trailer
Vorspann, Vorspanntitel – credits, credit title, leader, main title, opening title, opening credits
vorsprechen – to speak for audition
Vorstellung – performance
Vorstellung des Regisseurs, wie er eine Szene auflösen will – director's plan for covering a scene
Vorverkauf – advance sale
Vorverstärker – pre-amplifier
Vorverstärkung – gain amplification
Vorwärtsgang – forward action
Vorwickelrolle – take-off drum, take-off roller, take-up carter

W

Wackelkontakt – unsteady contact
während der Belichtung zoomen – zooming in the course of exposure
Wanderkino – touring cinema
Wandermaske – traveling mask, traveling matte
Wandertitel – moving title
Wandler von Gleichstrom auf Wechselstrom – inverter
warme Farben – warm colors
Wärmeschutzfilter – heat-absorbing glass
Wartung – maintenance
Wasserfleck – water stain
wässern – to rinse, to wash
Wässerung – rinsing
Wasserwaage – spirit level
Wechselmagazin – quick-change magazine
Wechselobjektiv – interchangeable lens system
Wechselsack – changing bag
Wechselstrom – a.c., alternating current
Wechselstromgenerator – a.c. generator
Wechselstromwiderstand – a.c. resistance
weiches Bromsilberpapier – soft bromide paper
Weichzeichnerobjektiv – soft focus lens
Weißabgleich – white balance
Weißabgleichanzeige – white balance indicator
Weißfilm – white film, white leader, white spacing, blank film
Weißpegel – carrier reference white level, picture white, white level
Weißwertbegrenzung – white clipping
Weitwinkelaufnahme – panorame
Weitwinkelbalgen – wide-angle bellows
Weitwinkeleffekt – wide-angle effect
Weitwinkelkompendium – wide-angle matte box
Weitwinkelobjektiv – wide-angle lens
Weitwinkelzoomobjektiv – wide-angle zoom lens
Wellenberg – wave crest
Wellenlänge – wavelength
Welturaufführung – world premier

Werbeeinblendung – advertising break, commercial
Werbefilm – advertising film, commercial
Werbefilm mit Laiendarstellern – testimonial
Werbefoto – advertising photo
Werbespot – commercial spot
Werbung – advertisement, commercial
Werkfoto – candid still
Western – wild west film
Wetterschutzhaube – rain cover, weather protector cover
wickeln – to wind
Wicklung – winding
Widerstand (als elektronisches Bauteil) – rheostat resistor
Widerstand (für Scheinwerfer) – dimmer
Wiederaufnahme eines Films ins Kinoprogramm – re-release
Wiedergabe – reproduction
Wiedergabekopf – pick-up head, playback head
Wiedergabequalität – quality of reproduction
Wiedergabeverstärker – play-back amplifier
Wiederholung einer Aufnahme – retake (US)
Wiederholung eines Films im Fernsehprogramm – re-run
Wiederholungsaufnahme, »die 2.« – re-take, reticulation
Wiederverfilmung – remake
winden – to wind
Windmaschine – ritter, wind machine
Windmuff – windsock
Windschutz – wind protection
Winkelblende – angle fade
Winkelgeschwindigkeit – angular speed
Winkelsucher – angle (view-) finder, offset view-finder
wirksame Öffnung – actual aperture, effective aperture
Wischblende – wipe
Wischer – flash pan, swish pan, whip pan, zip pan
Wobbelfrequenz – sweep frequency
Wochenschau – news-reel
Wochenschaukameramann – news-reel cameraman

X

X-Achse, Zeitbasis – time-base
Xenonkopie – xenon print
Xenonlampe – xenon lamp
Xenonprojektor – xenon projector
X-Kontakt – X-contact

Z

Zahlenfächer – pocket ident
Zählwerk – counter
Zahnkranz – gear ring
Zahntrommel – sprocket
Zebraröhre – index tube
10kW Lampe – tenner
Zeichentrickfilm – animated cartoon
Zeiger – pointer
Zeilen (ablenk) transformator – line output transformer
Zeilenablenkeinheit – line scanning unit
Zeilenablenkung – horizontal sweep
Zeilenabstand – line spacing
Zeilenabtastdauer – trace interval
Zeilenabtastung – line scanning, raster scan
Zeilenaustastimpulse – line blanking pulse
Zeilenaustastlücke – line blanking interval
Zeilenaustastung – horizontal blanking
Zeilenbreite – line width
Zeilenbreitenregler – horizontal size control
Zeileneinschwinger – scan ring
Zeilenendstufentransistor – horizontal scan output transistor
Zeilenendtrafo – flyback trafo
Zeilenentzerrung – line bend, line tilt
Zeilenfangregler – horizontal hold, line hold
Zeilenflimmern – line flicker, line jitter, line shake
zeilenfrei – line-free, spot-wobbled
Zeilenfrequenz – horizontal frequency, horizontal power, line frequency
Zeilengleichlaufsignal – line sync signal
Zeilenimpuls – line sync puls, line synchronisation impulse
Zeileninhalt – scanning spots of a line
Zeilenkippgenerator – horizontal time-base generator
Zeilenkippschaltung – line scan circuit
Zeilenkippspannung – line-scanning voltage
Zeilennorm – line standard
Zeilenrauschen – low frequency noise

Zeilenrücklauf – horizontal flyback, horizontal retrace
Zeilenschlupf – line slip
Zeilenspratzer – line jitter
Zeilensprung – interlaced scanning, line interlacing
Zeilensprungverfahren – line-jump scanning, interlaced scanning, line interlace, progressive interlace
Zeilensteuerung – line control
Zeilensynchronimpuls – line sync puls, line synchronisation impulse
Zeilensynchronisation – line lock
Zeilenversatz, Zeilenwandern – line pulling
Zeilenwechselfrequenz – line frequency
zeilenweises Abtasten – line scanning, raster scan
Zeilenzahl – definition
zeitabhängiger Kippgenerator – time base generator
Zeitablenkschaltung – sweep circuit
Zeitablenkspannung – sweep voltage, timebase voltage
Zeitablenkung – time base, time-base deflection, X-deflection
Zeitbasis – time-base
Zeitfehlerkorrektur – time-base corrector
zeitgenössische Musik – period music
zeitgenössisches Kostüm – period costume
Zeitlupe – slow motion
Zeitlupenkamera – high-speed camera
Zeitlupenscheibe – slo-mo disk
Zeitraffer – accelerated motion, fast-motion, quick motion, stop motion, time accelerator, time-lapse, undercrank
Zeitrafferaufnahme – time lapse shooting, to shoot with low speed
Zeitraffer-Videorekorder – time lapse recorder
Zeitungsausschnitt – cutting, clipping
Zeitungsinserat – advertisement, publicity
Zeitvertrag – unestablished staff contract
Zensurkopie – censor copy
Zentralarchiv – main reference library
Zentraldisposition – production planning department
Zentralschärfe – definition of the centre
Zentralstrahl – central ray
Zentralverschluß – central shutter, leaf shutter
Zeppelin (*slang*) – zeppelin, zeppelin windscreen

Zerrlinse – anamorphoser
Zerstreuungskreis – circle of confusion, coma
Zerstreuungslinse – diverging lens
Zimmerantenne – rabbit ears (*slang*)
zischen – frying
Zischlaut – sibilants
Zittern – jitter
Zoomantrieb – servo zoom drive
zoomen – to zoom
zoomen, aufziehen, aufziehende Aufnahme, die Brennweite verkürzen – zoom-away shot, zoom-out shot
zoomen, verdichten, verdichtende Aufnahme, die Brennweite verlängern – zoom-in shot
Zoomhebel – zoom handle, zoom lever, zoom rod
Zoomobjektiv – transfocator, variofocal lens, zoom-lens
Zoomobjektiv mit elektrischem Antrieb – power zoom
Zubehör – accessory, fittings
Zubehörschuh – accessory shoe, T-shoe
Zubehörtasche des Kameraassistenten – ditty bag
zu geringe Aussteuerung – undermodulation
zu geringe Aussteuerung – undermodulation
zu kontrastreich – too contrasty, snoot and white wash (*slang*)
zu kontrastreich – too contrasty, snoot and white wash (*slang*)
zulässige Spannung – allowable voltage
zu laut – blasting
Zurückfahrt mit anschließender Heranfahrt auf ein Motiv – double move
zurückschneiden in eine Szene, die durch einen Zwischenschnitt unterbrochen wurde – to cut back
Zusammenfassung – glossary
Zusatzgerät – gadgets
Zusatzlicht – booster light, fill light
Zusatzlinse – additional lens, supplementary lens
Zusatzlösung – additive
Zuschauer – patron, viewer
Zuschlag an Sonn- und Feiertagen – double time
zuschlagpflichtige Sonn- und Feiertage – golden times
zuspielen – to earn

Zuspielrekorder – slave recorder
zweiäugige Spiegelreflexkamera – twin-lens reflex camera
Zweibadentwickler – two-bath developer
Zweibandaufnahmeverfahren – double system
Zweibandprojektor – sound picture projector, two track projector
2-Ebenenbildmischer – A-B-C-D cut mixer
Zweiereinstellung – two-shot
Zweiflügelblende – two-blades shutter
2kW Leuchte – junior
2kW Stufenlinsenscheinwerfer – deuce (*slang*)
Zweiraumkassette – coaxial magazine
2-Stufenbildmischer – A-B-C-D cut mixer
Zweitausstrahlung – second showing
Zweitbelichtung – re-exposure
»die 2.«, eine Aufnahme wiederholen – reticulation
2. Korrekturkopie – second answer print
zweiter Aufnahmeleiter – assistant u.p.m. (under production manager)
zweiter Tonassistent – boom operator
zweites Team – second unit
Zwillingsobjektiv – twin lens
Zwischenbild-Ikonoskop – super iconoscope
Zwischenduplikat – intermediate dup
Zwischenflügel einer Umlaufblende – cover blade, cutting blade, intercepting blade, intermediate blade, two blade shutter, anti-flicker blade of a rotating shutter
Zwischenfrequenz – intermediate frequency
Zwischenlinsenverschluß – between-the-lens shutter
Zwischennegativ – intermediate negative, internegative
Zwischenprogramm – filler (US)
Zwischenpunktflimmern – interdot flicker
Zwischenring – extension tube
Zwischenschnitt – bridge, buffer shot, continuity shot, cutaway, insert, intercut, pick-up
Zwischenspannung – interlace
Zwischentitel – title-link, information caption
Zwischenträger – subcarrier

englisch – deutsch

A

A and B printing – A/B Kopierverfahren
Abby singer shot (*slang*) – vorletzte Einstellung eines Drehtags
A-B-C-D cut mixer – 4-Ebenenbildmischer, Zweistufenbildmischer
A-B cut mixer – 2-Ebenenbildmischer, Einstufenbildmischer
aberration – Aberration, Abweichung
aberration defect – Abbildungsfehler
aberration free – aberrationsfrei
above-the-line costs – Kosten innerhalb einer Filmkalkulation für die kreativen Mitarbeiter
A-B powered microphone – tonadergespeistes Mikrofon
abraisions – Schrammen und Kratzer auf einem Film, die durch Filmsalat verursacht werden
absence of flicker – flimmerfrei
to absorb – absorbieren, streuen
abrasion – Abschürfung
absorption filter – Absorptionsfilter
abstract set (US) – Studiodekor
academy format film gate – Bildfenster für Normalfilmformat
academy format ground glass – Mattscheibe mit Normalfilmformat-Markierung
accelerated motion – Zeitraffer
accentuation filter – Anhebungsfilter
acceptance angle – Aufnahmewinkel, Meßfeld
accessory – Zubehör
accessory shoe – Zubehörschuh
accident in working – Betriebsunfall
account of expenses – Spesenabrechnung
accuracy of color value – Tonwertrichtigkeit von Farben
ace – 1kW Stufenlinsenscheinwerfer
acetate base film – Acetatfilm
acetate film – Acetatfilm
a.c. generator – Wechselstromgenerator
achromate – Achromat
achromatic, achromatically – achromatisch, farbfehlerfrei, farblos, unbunt
achromatic lens – achromatisches Objektiv, Achromat
achromatic locus – Unbuntbereich

achromatic sensation – Grauempfindung
achromatism – Achromatismus, farblos
acouity of color image – Farbauflösungsvermögen
acoustical back coupling – akustische Rückkopplung
acoustical efficiency – akustischer Wirkungsgrad
acoustical engineering – Tontechnik
acoustical feedback – akustische Rückkopplung
acoustical feedback – Pfeifen, Rückkopplung
acoustical field – Schallfeld
acoustical impedance – akustischer Scheinwiderstand
acoustically dead – schalltot
acoustical oscillation – akustische Schwingung
acoustical output – Schalleistung
acoustical perception – Tonempfindung
acoustical power – Schalleistung
acoustical reproduction – Tonwiedergabe
acoustical resistance – akustischer Scheinwiderstand
acoustical short circuit – akustischer Kurzschluß
acoustical source – Schallquelle
acoustics – Akustik, Lehre vom Schall
to acquire – kaufen
acquisition of rights – Erwerb von Rechten
a.c. pick-up – Netzbrummen
a.c. power supply – Netzgerät
a.c. resistance – Wechselstromwiderstand
a.c. ripple voltage – Brummspannung
action of light – Lichteinwirkung
»Action! Start grinding!« – »Achtung! Aufnahme!« Anweisung an den Kameramann
action still – Vergrößerung eines Filmbilds
action track – stumme Filmkopie
to act opposite the star – als Partner des Hauptdarstellers spielen
actor – Darsteller, Schauspieler
actor without expression – ausdrucksloser Schauspieler
actress – Darstellerin, Schauspielerin
actual aperture – wirksame Blendenöffnung
actual grey-value – grauwertrichtig
acuity – Schärfe

acuity of color definition – Farbauflösungsvermögen
acutance – Konturenschärfe
acuteness of color definition (US) – Farbauflösungsvermögen
adaptation by... – angepaßt von... (im Titel)
adaptation of a novel – Romanbearbeitung
adaptator – Bearbeiter
adaption – Bearbeitung
additional film – Beifilm, Beiprogramm
additional lens – Hilfslinse, Vorsatzlinse, Zusatzlinse
additional mirror – Hilfsspiegel
additive – Zusatzlösung
additive color process – additives Farbverfahren
to add sound to a film – vertonen
adhesive tape – Lassoband
adjacent channel selectivity – Trennschärfe
adjacent picture carrier, adjacent vision carrier – Nachbarbildträger
adjacent picture carrier spacing – Bildträgerabstand
adjustable counter balance spring – einstellbare Gewichtsausgleichfeder
adjustable timer – Schaltuhr
adjusting knobs – Feststellschrauben
adjusting screw – Justierschraube
adjustment – Abgleich, Einstellung
adjustment facility – Verstellweg
ad lip – live ohne üben
admission fee – Eintrittspreis
admission tax – Vergnügungssteuer
advance – Ton/Bildversatz
advance payment – Vorauszahlung
advance sale – Vorverkauf
adventure film – Abenteuerfilm
advertisement – Anzeige, Werbung, Zeitungsinserat
advertising break – Werbeeinblendung
advertising film – Werbefilm
advertising photo – Werbeaufnahme
ad writer – Texter
aerial element – Antennenelement
aerial equipment – Ausrüstung für Luftbildaufnahmen
aerial frame – Rahmenantenne

aerial image – virtuelles Bild
aerial input – Antenneneingang
aerial output – Antennenausgang
aerial photography – Luftaufnahme
aerial signal – Antennensignal
aerial view – Luftbild
A.F. amplifier – Niederfrequenzverstärker, NF-Verstärker
A.F. filter – NF-Filter
after glow – Nachleuchten, Nachleuchtdauer
after-image – Nachbild, Nachziehen
agency – Agentur
aging – Alterung
to agitate – schütteln
agitation – Bewegung
to air – senden , über den Sender gehen
air gap in the magnetic head – Luftspalt (im Magnettonkopf)
air-glass interface – Luft-Glas Grenzfläche
air-tight metal box – luftdichte Metallbüchse
air time – Sendezeit
air-to-air – Luft-Luftaufnahme
albumen lazur – Eiweißlasur
to align a projector – einen Projektor ausrichten
alignment – Abgleich
alignment of heads – Einmessen der Köpfe
alkaline metal-cell – Alkalizelle
all bottom sound – dumpfer, dunkler Ton
alligator grip, alligator cramp – Krokodilklemme
allochroism – Farbwechsel
allowable voltage – zulässige Spannung
all-wave reciever – UKW Empfänger
alteration of current – Spannungsänderung
alternating burst – alternierender Burst
alternating current – Wechselstrom
alternating magnetic field – magnetisches Wechselfeld
alto, alto-singer – Altist
alto, alto voice – Altstimme
aluminum camera case – Aluminiumkamerakoffer
ambience – Ambiente

ambient air – umgebende Luft
ambient light – Raumlicht
ammeter – Ampèremeter
amperage – Stromstärke
ampere-hour – Ampèrestunde
amplification – Verstärkung
amplifier output voltage – Verstärkerausgangsspannung
to amplify – verstärken
amplifying factor – Verstärkungsfaktor
amplitude-frequency response – Frequenzgang
amplitude increase – Ampltitudenaufschaukelung
amplitude modulation – Amplitudenmodulation, AM
amplitude separation circuit, amplitude separation lopper – Amplitudenbegrenzer, Amplitudenunterdrücker
amplitude variations – Amplitudenschwankungen
anachromatic lens – Anachromat, anachromatisches Objektiv
anaglyphe – Anaglyph
anaglyphe process – Anaglyphenverfahren
anaglyphe spectacles – Anaglyphenbrille
analysis of color – Farbanalyse
anamorphose – Bildverzerrung
anamorphoser – Verzerrungslinse, Zerrlinse
anamorphotic attachment – anamorphotische Einrichtung
anamorphotic lens – Anamorphot, anamorphotisches Objektiv
anamorphotic mirror – anamorphotischer Spiegel
anamorphotic squeezed negative – anamorphotisch gepreßtes Negativ
anamorphotic system – anamorphotisches System
anarmorphoze lens – anamorphotisches Objektiv
anastigmat – Anastigmat
anastigmatic lens – anastigmatisches Objektiv
anastigmatism – Anastigmatismus
anchor man – Moderator, Studioredakteur
ancillary room – Nebenraum
anechoic room – schalltoter Raum
angle fade-in – Winkelaufblende
angle fade-out – Winkelabblende
angle finder – Winkelsucher
angle of coverage – Bildkreisdurchmesser

angle of deflection – Ausfallswinkel
angle of emergence – Austrittswinkel
angle of incidence – Einfallswinkel
angle of projection – Projektionswinkel
angle of radiation – Abstrahlwinkel
angle of reflection – Reflexionswinkel
angle of view – Bildwinkel
angle view-finder – Winkelsucher
angular field – Bildwinkel
angular geared base – Umlenkgetriebe
angular speed – Winkelgeschwindigkeit
to animate a dead scene – eine Spielfilmszene durch Statisten beleben
animated camera – Einzelbildkamera
animated camera trigger – Tricktaste
animated caption – Tricktitel
animated cartoon – Trickfilm, Zeichentrickfilm
animated mixer – Trickmischer
animated screen camera – Trickkamera
animated stand – Tricktisch
animated superimposition – Tricküberblendung
animated viewer – Laufbildbetrachter
animator – Trickfilmzeichner
announcer studio – Sprecherraum
anode characteristic – Röhrenkennlinie
answer print – Nullkopie
antenna – Antenne
antenna diplexer – Antennenweiche
antenna element – Antennenelement
antenna input – Antenneneingang
antenna mast – Antennenmast
antenna matching – Antennenabstimmung
antenna output – Antennenausgang
antenna pick-up – Antennenanschluß
antenna reception – Empfang über Antenne
antenna rotor – Antennenrotor
antenna signal – Antennensignal
antenna two-way splitter – Antennenweiche
anterior shutter – Objektivblende, Vorderblende

anti-firing regulations – Sicherheitsvorschriften
anti-flicker blade (vane) of a rotating shutter – Beruhigungsflügel eines Umlaufverschlusses
anti-fog agent – Antischleiermittel
antihalation – Lichthofschutz
antihalation layer – Lichthofschutzschicht
anti-halo – lichthoffrei
anti-parallax mirror – Spiegel für den Parallaxenausgleich
antireflex layer of a lens – Antireflexbelag einer Linse, Vergütung
aperture – Apertur, Blendenöffnung, Bildfenster
aperture compensating, aperture correction (GB) – Aperturkorrektur
aperture diaphragm error – Aperturblendenfehler
aperture disk – Nipkowscheibe
aperture equalization (US) – Aperturkorrektur
aperture mask – Lochmaske
aperture plate – Bildfenster
aperture stop – Blende
aplanat – Aplanat
apochromat – Apochromat
apparatus room – Bildregieraum
apparent sharpness – Konturenschärfe
apple box – Bühnenkiste, Plattform für Schauspieler
approval print – Nullkopie
architectural view – Architekturaufnahme
arcing – Bogenkamerafahrt
arc lamp – Bogenlampe
area of the picture – Bildfeld
arranger – Arrangeur
art board – Titelkarton
art director – Bühnenbildner, Filmarchitekt
art film – Kurzfilm
artificial aging – künstliche Alterung
artificial black signal – Testsignal für Schwarz
artificial-light shot – Kunstlichtaufnahme
artificial white signal – Testsignal für Weiß
artist's dressing-room – Künstlergarderobe
arts feature editor – Kulturredakteur
A.S.A. speed – Filmempfindlichkeit nach ASA

ashan – 1000W Scheinwerfer
aspect ratio – Bild-Seitenverhältnis
assembly – Rohschnitt
assistant cameraman – Kameraassistent
assistant director – Regieassistent
assistant u.p.m. (under production manager) – zweiter Aufnahmeleiter
associate director – Co-Regisseur
associate producer – Produktionsleiter
astigmatism – Astigmatismus
asymmetrical anastigmat – asymetrischer Anastigmat
asynchronous motor – Asynchronmotor
A-team – 1. Team
atmosphere vehicle – Fahrzeug, das von Komparsen verwendet wird
atmospherics – Rundfunkstörungen
attack time – Ansprechzeit für Limiter
attenuation – Pegelvordämpfung
audible distortion – hörbare Verzerrung
audible frequency – hörbarer Frequenzbereich
audience – Publikum
audience rating – Messung der Sehbeteiligung
audiobroadcasting – Rundfunksendung
audiofrequency channel – Tonkanal
audio head – Tonkopf
audiomixer – Tonmischpult
audio oscillator – Tongenerator
audio signal – Tonsignal
audiovisual aids – audiovisuelle Unterrichtsmittel
auditorium acoustics – Theaterakustik
aural signal – Tonsignal
author – Autor
author's rights – Urheberrecht
autofocus – automatische Scharfstellung
auto iris – automatische Blendensteuerung
auto locator – Bandsuchlauf
automatic aperture control – automatische Blendensteuerung
automatic brightness control – automatische Helligkeitsregelung
automatic diaphragm – automatische Springblende, Spingblende
automatic gain control – automatische Verstärkungsschaltung

automatic locking circuit – automatische Synchronisationsschaltung
automatic peak limiting – automatische Weißwertbegrenzung
automatic phase control – automatische Phasenregelung
automatic volume control – automatische Lautstärkeregelung
automobile base – Autostativ
auto timer – Selbstauslöser
available light – verfügbares Licht, vorhandenes Licht
available light photography – Aufnahmen mit vorhandenem Licht, Restlichtfotografie
average picture level – durchschnittliche Bildhelligkeit
average value – Mittelwert
award – Auszeichnung, Diplom, Preis
azimuthal alignment tape – Testband zur Einstellung der Spaltöffnung beim Magnetkopf

B

baby – Kamera (*slang*)
baby legs – Babystativ
baby spot – 1/2kW Lampe
backdrop – Prospekt (*Hintergrund*)
back focus – Auflagemaß
background – Hintergrund
background music – untermalende Musik
background projection – Rückpro
backing – Hintergrund
backlight – Gegenlicht (außen)
back lot – Studioaußengelände
back porch – Austastschulter
back projection – Durchprojektion
back standard – hintere Standarte
baffle – Schallschutzwand
balanced microphone input – symetrischer Mikrofoneingang
balanced print – lichtbestimmte Kopie
balance plate – Nivellierplatte
balance stripe – Magnettonausgleichsspur auf Filmkopien
balance wheel – Schwungrad
ball-and-socket head – Kugelgelenkkopf
ballast – Vorschaltgerät für HMI-Lampen
ballet feature – Ballettfilm
band – Frequenzband
band expansion, band spread – Banddehnung
band width – Bandbreite
bank, bank of lamps – Flächenleuchte
banned film – indizierter Film
to bare the wires – Kabel abisolieren
bar generator – Farbbalkengeber
barndoor – Lampentor, Lichtblende, Scheunentor (*slang*), Torblende
barney – Schallschutzhaube
barrel distortion – tonnenförmige Verzeichnung
barrier layer – Sperrschicht
base – Filmunterlage, Trägermaterial
baseboard camera – Laufbodenkamera

based on a story by ... – nach einem Roman von ...
basher – Augenlicht, Fluter, Kopflicht
basked windshield – Korbwindschutz, Zeppelin (*slang*)
bass boost – Tiefenanhebung
bass cut filter – Tiefenfilter
bass cut filtering – Tiefenabsenkung
bass system – Tieftonsystem
battery – Akku, Batterie
battery belt – Akkugürtel
battery check – Batteriekontrolle
battery lighting – Akkulicht
bayonet closing – Bajonettanschluß
bayonet mount – Bajonettfassung
bazooka – Aufhängvorrichtung für Lampen auf der Beleuchterbrücke
beam antenna – Richtantenne
beam current – Strahlstrom
beam deflection – Strahlablenkung
beam focus – Strahlschärfe
beam gate – Strahlunterdrückung
beam splitter – Strahlenteilungsprisma
beam suppression – Strahlaustastung beim Rücksprung
bear trap – Krokodilklemme
beat – Interferenz
beat frequency – Schwebungsfrequenz
beginner – Anfänger
bellow extension of camera – Balgenauszug
bellows – Balgen
bellows matte box – Balgenkompendium
bench camera – Trickkamera
to be on the air – ausstrahlen, senden
best boy – Hilfskraft
best view – bester Visus, optimales Sehvermögen
between-the-lens shutter – Zwischenlinsenverschluß
bias – Gitterspannung, Vorspannung
bias light – Auflicht, Biaslicht
big close up – sehr große Einstellung
big eye – 100kW Scheinwerfer
to bill – terminieren, zeitlich abstimmen
billing – Erwähnung der Namen der Mitarbeiter

bin – Abfalleimer
bird's eye view – Vogelperspektive
bit player – Kleindarsteller
black-and-white – schwarzweiß
black-and-white film – Schwarzweißfilm
black body – Planckscher Strahler, schwarzer Körper
black clipping – Schwarzwertbegrenzung
black leader – Schwarzfilm, Schwarzfilmvorspann
black level – Schwarzpegel, Schwarzwert
black-level clamping – Schwarzwertklemmung
blackout (US) – Austastung
to black out – abblenden
blackout of video signal – Austastung des Bildsignals
blackout signal – Austastsignal
black peak (US) – maximaler Schwarzwert
black reference level – Bezugspegel für Schwarz
Black Rock – Spitzname für das CBS Verwaltungsgebäude
black stretch – Schwarzwertanhebung
Black Tower – Spitzname für das Verwaltungsgebäude der Universal Pictures, Ca.
black track print – Nullkopie ohne Lichtton
to blank – austasten
blanket rig – Pantograf, an dem im Studio die Scheinwerfer hängen
blank film – Weißfilm
blanking (GB) – Austastung
blanking during flyback – Strahlaustastung beim Rücksprung
blanking pulse – Vertikalaustastimpuls
blanking signal – Austastsignal
to blast – übersteuern
blasting – Übersteuert, zu laut
bleach – Bleichbad
bleached out – ausgefressen, überbelichteter Film
bleach fix, bleach fixing bath – Bleichfixierbad
to bleach out – ausbleichen
blimp – Schallschutzgehäuse
blocking bias – Sperrspannung
blocking layer – Sperrschicht
bloom – Überstrahlung
bloomed lens – vergütetes Objektiv

blooming – Überstrahlung
bloop – Klebestellengeräusch, Tonblubbern
blow-up – fotografische Vergrößerung
blue – Blau
blue apex – Farbort der blauen Primärfarbe
blue-color difference signal – B-Y Signal
blue-color matrix difference – B-Y Matrix
blue filter – Blaufilter
blue-green filter – Blaugrünfilter
blue overcast – blaustich
blue-print – Blaupause, Lichtpause
blue-printing frame – Lichtpausapparat
blue-print paper – Lichtpauspapier
blue sensitive – blauempfindlich
blue shading, blue tinged, bluish tinged – blaustichig
blurred – flau, kontrastlos, unscharf, weich
blurring – Unschärfe
B-movie – low-budget Film
bob, bobby – Bobby, Filmbobby, Filmkern
body – Kameragehäuse
body brace – Schulterstütze
bone-glass – Opalglas
booker – Disponent, Disponentin
boom – Kamera- oder Mikrofonkran
boom operator – Tonangler, zweiter Tonassistent
booster amplifier – Endverstärker, Hauptverstärker
booster light – **Aufheller, Aufhellicht, Außenaufhellung, Zusatzlicht**
booth – Projektionsraum
bottom loop – untere Filmschleife
bounced light – indirektes Licht
bouncing – Bildpumpen, senkrechte Bildlageschwankung, Rucken über H
box office – Abendkasse
box-office record – Kassenrekord
brake of the film-run – Filmlaufbremse, Friktion
Braun tube – Braunsche Röhre
break-down of rushes – Muster trennen
breaked idler roller – Vorberuhigungsrolle
breast-tripod – Bruststütze
breezing – Unschärfe

bridge – Schnittbild, Zwischenschnitt
brightening screen, brighting screen – Aufheller, Aufhellwand
brightness contrast – Helligkeitskontrast
brightness of the image spot – Bildpunkthelligkeit
brightness range – Kontrastumfang
bright view-finder – heller Sucher
brilliance of the image spot – Bildpunkthelligkeit
brilliancy – Brillanz
brilliant finder, brilliant view-finder – Durchsichtsucher
broad – Soffite
broadcast – Rundfunk
broadcasting house – Funkhaus, Sendeanstalt
broadcasting time – Sendezeit
broadcast interference – Rundfunkstörung
broadcast studio – Rundfunkstudio
broad source, broad – Lichtwanne
bromide paper – Bromsilberpapier
to brown – brünieren
brute – HI Lampe
buckle – Filmschlaufe
budget breakdown – Kostenvoranschlag
buffer shot – Schnittbild, Zwischenschnitt
bugeye – Fischaugenobjektiv
bulb – Brenner, Glühbirne
bulk eraser – Löschdrossel
bulky luggage – Sperrgepäck
to bunch the light – das Licht bündeln
burned-in image – Nachbild
burn-in – Einbrennstelle in der Aufnahmeröhre, Untertitel
to burn out – durchbrennen
burst – Burst, Farbsynchronsignal
burst phase – Hilfsträgerphase des Farbsynchronsignals
bush – Stativmutter
butt joiner – Stumpfklebepresse, Stumpfklebelade
butt splice – Stumpfklebestelle
B-Y matrix – B-Y Matrix
bypass – Parallelschaltung
B-Y signal – B-Y Signal

C

cabin window – Projektionsraumfenster

cable correction, cable length compensation, cable length equilisation – Kabellängenausgleich

cable duct – Kabelkanal

cable grip, cableman, cable person, cable puller – Kabelhilfe

cable reception – Empfang über Kabel, Kabelanschluß

cable reel – Kabeltrommel

cable release – Drahtauslöser

cafeteria – Kantine

calibration – Eichung, Kalibrierung

calibration reel – Bezugsband, Einstellfilm, Meßfilm

calibrator – Eichgenerator

Callier's effect, Callier's quotient – Callier-Effekt, Callier-Faktor

callsign – Rufzeichen

camcorder – Rekorderkamera

camera – Kamera

»Camera! Action!« – »Achtung, Aufnahme!«

camera balancing – Kameragewichtsausgleich

camera body – Kameragehäuse

camera car – Teamwagen, Kamerawagen

camera case – Bereitschaftstasche

camera control room – Bildregieraum

camera coverage – Bildfeld, Gesichtsfeld

camera crane – Kamerakran

camera direction – Kameraeinstellung

camera dolly – Dolly, Kamerawagen

camera for standard film – Normalfilmkamera

camera headlamp, camera light – Augenlicht, Frontaufheller, Kopflicht

camera lines – Auflösungsvermögen

cameraman – Kameramann, Schwenker

camera marker – Synchronklappe

camera master – belichteter Film, der durch die Kamera lief

camera noise – Laufgeräusch der Filmkamera

camera operator – 1. Kameraassistent, Schwenker

camera roll – Filmmagazin

camera set-up – elektronischer Kameraabgleich, Einstellung

camera sheet – Bildaufnahmebericht, Negativbericht
camera slide – Verstellplatte
camera stock – belichteter Film, der durch die Kamera lief
camera talk – Aufsager in die Kamera
camera trap – Sprungwand
can – 1. kW Strahler; Filmbüchse; Kopfhörer
candid still – Werkfoto
capstan – Bandantriebsachse, Bandtransportrolle
caption – Titelinsert, Text zu einem Bild, Untertitel
captions – Grafik
caption stand – Titelständer
to cap-up – abdecken der Kameraröhren
carbon arcs – Kohlebogen
car for reportage and topicals – Reportagewagen, Ü-Wagen
car mount – Autostativ
carnet – Carnet
carrier – Träger
carrier difference system – Differenzträgerverfahren
carrier frequency – Trägerfrequenz
carrier reference white level – Weißpegel
carrying case – Koffer
carrying strap – Trageriemen
cartoon camera – Trickkamera
cartoon camera bench – Tricktisch
cartridge – Filmpatrone
case-hardening – Oberflächenhärtung
cash – Kasch, Maske, Vignette
cast – Besetzung, Ensemble, Rollenbesetzung, Schauspieltruppe
to cast – Rollen besetzen, Schauspieler engagieren
castered skid – Fahrspinne
cast shadow – Schlagschatten
cathode-ray tube – Braunsche Röhre, Kathodenstrahlröhre
cathode-ray tube persistence characteristic – Nachleuch-tcharakteristik einer Kathodenstrahlröhre
catwalk – Beleuchterbrücke
cell – Phase, Trickfilmphase
cell of an accumulator – Akkumulatorzelle

celluloid scratch – Blankschramme
to cement – einkitten, verkitten
cement – Filmkleber
cemented lens – Objektiv mit verkitteten Linsen
cemented lenses – verkittete Linsen
censor copy – Zensurkopie
center of picture – Bildmitte
central apparatus room – Bild- und Tonschaltraum
central ray – Zentralstrahl
central shutter – Zentralverschluß
change of program – Programmwechsel
change of scene – Szenenwechsel
change-over – Passage, Überblendung
change-over cue, change-over mark, change-over signal – Überblendzeichen
change-over switch – Betriebsartenumschalter
to change the tape – das Band wechseln
changing bag – Dunkelsack, Kassettenwechselsack, Wechselsack
channel – Kanal, Mischpulteingang, Toneingang
channel conversion – Kanalumsetzer
channel spacing – Kanalabstand
character – Darsteller, Schauspieler, Zeichen
character actor – Charakterdarsteller
character generator – Schriftgeber
characteristic curve – Schwärzungskurve
charge – Ladung, Speisung
charge image (GB) – Ladungsbild
charger – Ladegerät
charge-storage tube – Speicherröhre
chart of the pictures in production, chart of the features in production – Produktionsspiegel
checkerboard pattern (US) – Schachbrettestbild
checkroom (US) – Garderobe
to check the gate – Fusselkontrolle des Filmfensters
cheese-cutter – Neger (*slang*), schwarze Wand
cherry picker – kleiner selbstfahrender Kran, Steiger
chessboard pattern (GB) – Schachbrettestbild

chief electrician – Oberbeleuchter
chief recorder (US) – Tonmeister
chinagraph, chinagraph wax pencil – Fettstift
china marker – Fettstift
chroma control – Farbregler
chroma-key – Farbschablonentrick
chroma-key backing – eingestanzter Hintergrund
chromatical aberration – chromatische Aberration, Farbfehler
chromatic fringe – Farbsaum
chromaticity – Farbton
chromatic selection – Farbauszug
chromatic sensitivity – Farbempfindlichkeit
chrome yellow – Chromgelb
chrominance – Farbwert
chrominance signal – Chrominanzsignal
cinch marks – Kratzer auf dem Film durch zu strammes Aufwickeln der Filmrolle
cine-camera – Filmkamera
cine-film – Film
cinema advertising – Kinowerbung
cinema technics – Kinotechnik
cinematography of medium with variable optical density – Schlierenkinematografie
cine-technical paper – filmtechnische Zeitung
cinetechnician – Filmtechniker
cinex strip – Farbteststreifen
circle of confusion – Zerstreuungskreis
circle of illumination – Bildkreisdurchmesser
circuit – Stromkreis
circuit diagram – Schaltplan
circuit plate – Platine
circuit termination – Leitungsabschluß
clapp, clapper, clapper board, clapp stick – Filmklappe, Klappe, Synchronklappe
clapperboy – Kameraassistent (der die Klappen schlägt)
clapper mark – Knacker (*slang*), Synchronmarke durch Klappe, Tonknacker
clarifying bath – Klärbad

claw – Greifer, Greiferantrieb
claw feed system – Greifersystem
claw movement – Greiferbewegung
to clean – reinigen
cleaning agent – Reinigungsmittel
clean tape – gelöschtes Band
»Clear camera!« – »Bitte das Bild frei machen!«
clearing bath – Klärbad
clear leader – Blankfilm
to clip – Film abklammern
clip lamp – Pinzalampe
clipping – Zeitungsausschnitt
clock – Takt
clockwork-motor camera – Kamera mit Federwerkmotor
close-down – Sendeschluß
»Closed set!« – Hinweisschild vor Studios, daß der Drehort nicht betreten werden darf
close medium shot – Halbtotale
close of transmission – Sendeschluß
close range – Naheinstellung
close shot – Großaufnahme
close-talking microphone – Nahbesprechungsmikrofon
to close the shutter – den Verschluß spannen
close-up – Großaufnahme
close-up focusing device – Naheinstellgerät
closing scene – Schlußeinstellung, Schlußszene
clothtape – Lassoband
cloudy streams – Schliere
C-mount adapter – C-Mount Adapter
to coach an actor in a part – einem Darsteller eine Rolle einstudieren
coarse grain – Grobkorn
coated lens – beschichtetes Objektiv
coating – Beschichtung, Schicht
coating tape – Schichtband
co-author – Mitautor
co-axial cable – Koaxialkabel
coaxial magazine – Zweiraumkassette
cobweb gun – Spinnwebmaschine

code notch – Kerbmarkierung
coil-cord – Spiralkabel
coiled power cord – Spiralstromkabel
coincidence adjusting pointer – Nachführzeiger
cold colors – kalte Farben
collecting lens – Sammellinse
collimator – Kollimator
color aberration – Farbabweichung
color balance – Farbbalance
color burst – Burst, Farbsynchronsignal
color cinex test – Farbbestimmungsprobe, Farbteststreifen
color control – Farbregler
color coordinate – Farbkoordinate
color corrected – farbkorrigiert
color correction – Farbkorrektur
color developer – Farbentwickler
color fidelity – Farbentreue
color film – Farbfilm
color filter disk – Farbfilterscheibe
color fringing – Farbsaum
color head – Farbmischkopf
color infra-red film – Infrarotfarbfilm
color master – Farborginalfilm (der durch die Kamera lief)
color picture tube of 110° – 110° Farbbildröhre
color print – Farbbild
color purity – Farbreinheit
color separation – Farbtrennung
color slide – Farbdia
color temperature – Farbtemperatur
color triangle – Farbdreieck
coma – Koma, Zerstreuungskreis
combination set of lenses – Satzobjektiv
combined print – Filmkopie mit Magnettonspur
combined recording-reproducing head – kombinierter Aufnahme-Wiedergabekopf, Sprech-Hörkopf
combo – Rekorderkamera
to come into shot – ins Bild kommen
comical film – komischer Film

commag (*Codewort*) – Filmkopie mit Magnettonspur
commentary – Filmkommentar, Kommentar
commentator's booth – Sprecherkabine
commentator's position – Sprecherplatz
commercial – Werbeeinblendung, Werbefilm
commercial spot – Werbespot
commissary – Kantine im Filmstudio
comopt (Codewort) – Film mit Lichttonspur
comparison test – Vergleichstest
compartment case – Universaltasche
compatibility – Kompatibilität
compensating developer – Ausgleichsentwickler
compensation of distortion – Entzerrung
compensation of parallax – Parallaxenausgleich
compensation of temperature – Temperaturausgleich
complementary color – Komplementärfarbe
complementary hue – komplementärer Farbton
to complete – abdrehen
component – Bauteil
composer – Komponist
composite print – Filmkopie mit Lichttonspur
compositer – Schriftgeber
composite shot – Einkopierung
composite signal – FBAS-Signal, Summensignal
composition photo – Fotomontage
compur shutter – Compurverschluß
concave – konkav
concave mirror reflector – Hohlspiegel
concavo-convex – konkav-konvex
concavo-convex lens – Meniskuslinse
condensor, condenser lens – Kondensor, Kondensorlinse
conditions of development – Entwicklungsvorschriften
conditions of payment – Zahlungsbedingungen
conductor – Dirigent, Kapellmeister
to connect – einschalten, einschleifen, verbinden
connecting scene, connection scene – Anschlußszene
connection cable – Anschlußkabel, Verbindungskabel
connector – Anschluß

constant speed motor – Selbstregelmotor
contact pressure – Bandandruck
contact print – Kontaktkopie
contact printer – Kontaktkopiermaschine
contemporaneous release – Ringstart eines Filmes
continuity – Drehbuch, Rohdrehbuch, Filmkontinuität
continuity director – Ablaufregisseur
continuity girl – Ateliersekretärin, Scriptgirl
continuity list – Schnittliste
continuity report – Aufnahmebericht (mit Details über Einstellung, Dekoration, Schauspieler, Maske der Darsteller, etc), Drehbericht
continuity shot – Zwischenschnitt
continuity studio – Sprecherstudio
continuous filmprinter – Durchlaufkopiermaschine
contour sharpness – Konturenschärfe
contrast – Kontrast
contrast delay – Kontrastabfall
contrast factor – Kontrastfaktor
contrast filter – Kontrastfilter
control desk – Regiepult
control grid – Steuergitter
control ring – Steuerring
control strip – Kontrollstreifen, Teststreifen
control track – Steuerspur
convergence – Konvergenz, Rasterdeckung
converging lens – Sammellinse
converging lines toward the top of the image, converging verticals – stürzende Linien
converter – Umformer
convertible film gate – auswechselbares Filmfenster
convertible lens – Wechselobjektiv
convex – konvex
convex lens – Sammellinse
cookie – Maske vor Scheinwerfern; Schablonenlichtblende
cool – Fernsehbild mit leichtem Blau- oder Grünstich
cooling – Kühlung
copper bit, copper bolt – Lötkolben
copy – Abzug

copy date, copy deadline – Redaktionsschluß
copying accessory – Reproduktionszubehör
copyright – Urheberrecht
cordless sync – Quarzpilottonverfahren
core – Bobby, Filmbobby, Filmkern
core of the bobbin – Spulenkern
cornea – Hornhaut (Auge)
corner detail – Kantenschärfe
corrected print – Korrekturkopie, Nullkopie
correct exposure – korrekte Belichtung
correcting lens – Korrekturlinse
co-star – Partner des Hauptdarstellers
cost of financing – Finanzierungskosten
costume adviser – Kostümberater
costume design – Kostümentwurf
costume designer – Kostümbildner
costume film – historischer Film
costume house – Kostümverleih
counter – Zählwerk
counter-clockwise – entgegen dem Uhrzeigersinn
cove – Hohlkehle
coverage – Empfangsbereich, Empfangsgebiet, Sendegebiet; Szenenauflösung
to cover a scene – eine Filmsequenz in Einstellungen auflösen
cover blade – Zwischenflügel einer Umlaufblende
covered image format – Bildformat
cover frame of the screen – Abdeckrahmen der Bildwand
cover-glass – Deckgläschen
cover shot – Übersichtsaufnahme
cps, cycles per second – Hertz
crabbing – seitliche Dollyfahrt
crabbing – seitliche Kamerafahrt
to crackle – prasseln
crackling – Prasseln
cradle head – Stativkopfschale
cradle suspension – Mikrofonaufhängung, Mikrofonhalterung
crane – Kran
crane operator – Kranfahrer

crank – Kurbel
to crank – drehen, kurbeln
to crank a film – einen Film drehen
crawl title – Rolltitel
crawl title – langsamer Rolltitel
cream – chamois
credits, credit titles – Nachspann, Vorspann
crew – Ensemble, Filmteam, Team
critical definition – größtmögliche Schärfe
crocodile clip – Krokodilklemme
to crop – aus dem Bildausschnitt aussparen
crossed dipole – Kreuzdipol
cross fade, cross dissolve – Tonüberblendung
cross-gamma pattern – Testbild für die Gammakorrektur
cross hairs – Fadenkreuz
crossing the line – Achssprung
cross light – Seitenlicht
cross-plot – Produktionsplan
cross-section – Querschnitt, Querschnittzeichnung
crosswheel – Malteserkreuz
crowd artist – Statist
crown glass – Kronglas
crowsfoot – Stativspinne
crystal – Quarz
crystal-controlled – quarzgesteuert
crystal controlled motor, crystal motor – Quarzmotor
crystal pick-up – Kristalltonabnehmer
cucaloris – Maske vor Scheinwerfern, um Schatten zu erzeugen
cue – Bildsuchlauf
cue cards – Neger
cue dot – Überblendzeichen
cue mark – Markierung, Überblendungszeichen
cue track – Steuerspur
cultural affairs editor – Kulturredakteur
cultural film – Kulturfilm
current – Strom
current feed – Stromspeisung
curtain – Vorhang

curvature of field – Bildfeldwölbung
curved rail – gebogene Schiene
»Cut!« – »Aus«, »Schnitt!« (Ende einer Szene)
cut – Ausschnitt, Filmschnitt
to cut – hart überblenden, umschneiden
cutaway – Schnittbild, Zwischenschnitt
cut-back – Rückblende
to cut back – in eine Szene zurückschneiden, die durch einen Zwischenschnitt unterbrochen wurde
cut-in – Schnittbilder
cut-in scene – Anschnitt
to cut on action, to cut on move – in der Bewegung schneiden
cut out – Verschnitt, Filmrest
cut-out switch – Notausschalter
cutter – Cutter, Cutterin
cutter for gelatin foil – Stanze für Gelatinefilterfolien
cutting – Zeitungsausschnitt
cutting bench – Schneidetisch
cutting bench rental – Schneideraummiete
cutting blade – Zwischenflügel einer Umlaufblende
cutting copy – geschnittene Arbeitskopie, Rohschnittkopie, Schnittkopie
cutting order – Schnittfolge
cutting point – Schnittpunkt
cutting ratio – Drehverhältnis
cutting room – Schneideraum
cutting-room log – Schnittliste
cyan – blaugrün
cycles per second – Hertz
cyc-light – Rampenlicht
cyclorama – Rundhorizont
cylindrical anamorphoser – anamorphotische Zylinderlinse
cylorama – Rundhorizont

D

dailies (US) – AK, Arbeitskopie, Bildmuster, Klatsche (*slang*), Muster
daily assembling – ausmustern
daily commentary – Tageskommentar
daily performance – tägliche Aufführung
to damp a room – einen Raum akustisch abdämpfen, schallisolieren
dance director – Choreograf
dark – dunkel
dark room – Dunkelkammer
dark spot signal – Schwarzsignal
data sheet – Pflichtenheft, Produktionsbericht
date recording system – Dateneinbelichtung
dawn – Dämmerung
day-for-night – amerikanische Nacht
daylight – Tageslicht
daylight loading spool – Tageslichtspule
daylight magazine – Tageslichtkassette
daylight-type fluorescent tube – Tageslichtleuchtstoffröhre
dead room – schalltoter Raum
deconstruction – Abbau, Rückbau
decor – Szenenbild
definition – Auflösung
definition of the centre – Mittenschärfe
definition of the picture – Bildschärfe
deflected beam – abgelenkter Strahl
deflecting electrodes – Ablenkplatte
deflection – Ablenkung, Zeilenzahl
deflection distortion – Ablenkfehler
deflector – Ablenkeinheit
deflector plate – Ablenkplatte
defoamer – Entschäumer
to defocus – Bild in die Unschärfe ziehen
defocus mix – Überblendung durch Unschärfe
to degauss – entmagnetisieren
delay – Verzögerung
delivery spool – Abwickelspule

Delta-L correction, Delta-L system – Delta-L Korrektur
to demagnetize – entmagnetisieren
demodulation of frequency modulation – FM-Demodulation
densitometry – Densitometrie
density – Dichte, Schwärzung
density of a positive – Positivschwärzung
density recorder – Lichttonkamera für Sprossenschrift
density wedge – Graukeil
deposit – Filmabrieb
deposit of dust – Staubablagerung
deposit of the film – Fusseln, Filmabsatz
depth-of-field – Schärfentiefe, Tiefenschärfe
depth-of-field indicators – Tiefenschärfeanzeige
depth-of-field scale – Tiefenschärfenskala
depth-of-field table – Tiefenschärfetabelle
depth-of-focus – Tiefenschärfe
desaturation – Verminderung der Farbsättigung
detection – Gleichrichtung
detective film – Kriminalfilm
detector – Gleichrichter
deuce – 2kW Stufenlinsenscheinwerfer
to develop – entwickeln
developer – Entwickler
developing – Entwicklung
developing agent – Entwicklungssubstanz
developing box – Entwicklungsdose
developing dish – Entwicklungsschale
developing reversal – Umkehrentwicklung
developing shot – Umfahrt
development – Entwicklung
deviation prism – Umlenkprisma
diagonal cut – schräge Tonschnittstelle
diagonal splice – schräge Klebestelle
dial – Skala
to dial – den Ton aussteuern
dialog director – Dialogregisseur
dialogue – Dialog
dialogue recording – Sprachaufnahme

dialogue scene – Sprachszene
diaphragm – Blende
diaphragm ring – Blendenring
differential focusing – die Schärfe auf einen Punkt legen, um andere Bildteile unscharf zu bekommen
diffraction – Beugung
diffusing screen – Mattscheibe, Streulichtschirm
digital display – Digitalanzeige
to dilute – verdünnen
dilution – Verdünnung
to dim – abdunkeln, verdunkeln
dimmer – Dimmer, Scheinwerferwiderstand
dinky-inky – 100W oder 200 W Spotscheinwerfer
diopter, diopter lens – Nahlinse, Vorsatzlinse
diopter lens – Nahlinse
dip and dunk processor – Filmentwicklungsmaschine
to direct – inszenieren, die Kamera einstellen, Regie führen
direct broadcast by satellite – direkte Satellitenübertragung
direct current – Gleichstrom
direction – Regie, Regieanweisung
directional effect – Richteffekt
directional microphone – Richtmikrofon
direction of dialogue – Dialogregie
direction of lighting – Lichtführung
direction writer – Dialogautor
director – Intendant, Regisseur
director's chair – Regiestuhl
director's plan for covering a scene – Vorstellung (Idee) des Regisseurs, eine Szene aufzulösen
director of photography – erster Kameramann, lichtsetzender Kameramann
director of programs – Programmdirektor
directors view-finder – Motivsucher
direct print – Kontaktkopie
direct reverse – Gegenschuß
direct scanning – punktförmige Abtastung
dirt – Fussel
dirt in the gate – Negativfussel
dirty dupe – Einlicht Schwarzweißmuster

discussion chairman – Moderator
dish development – Schalenentwicklung
display – Anzeige, Anzeigeinstrument, Sichtgerät
dissolve – Überblendung
dissolve-in – Aufblende
distance between lens vertex and back focus – Schnittweite
distance between sound and image – Bild-Ton Versatz
distance setting – Entfernungseinstellung
distance shot – Totale
distortion, distortion factor, distortion percentage – Klirrfaktor, Verzerrung
distortionsfree – verzerrungsfrei
distributer – Verleiher
distributing amplifier – Antennenverstärker
distribution board – Schalttafel
distribution box – Mehrfachsteckdose
distribution company – Verleihfirma
distribution contract – Verleihvertrag, Verwertungsvertrag
distribution rights – Auswertungsrechte
ditty bag – Zubehörtasche des Kameraassistenten
diverging lens – Zerstreuungslinse
documentary – Dokumentarfilm
documentary cameraman – Dokumentarfilmkameramann
dolly – Dolly, Kamerawagen
dolly grip – Dollyfahrer
dollyshot, dollying shot – Fahraufnahme vom Kamerawagen
doorway dolly – kleiner Kamerawagen
dope sheet – Negativbericht, Bildaufnahmebericht
dot – kleine Lichtblende
double anastigmat – Doppelanastigmat
double concave – bikonkav
double condenser – Doppelkondensor
double conus – Doppelkonus
double exposure – Doppelbelichtung
double-exposure (prevention) lock – Doppelbelichtungssperre
double-face tape – doppelseitigklebendes Klebeband
double-head continuous contact printer – Durchlaufkopiermaschine für Bild und Lichtton

double image – Doppelbild
double move – Zurückfahrt und anschließende Heranfahrt auf ein Motiv
double register pin – doppelseitiger Sperrgreifer
double system – Zweibandaufnahmeverfahren
double time – Zuschlag an Sonn- und Feiertagen
dovetail – Schwalbenschwanz
down stage – in Richtung der Kamera
downstage – im vorderen Teil der Bühne
downstage – Bühnen-oder Dekorationsvordergrund
draft script – Treatment
to drain – abtropfen
dressing props – Kostümrequisiten
dressing-room (GB) – Garderobe
dress rehersal – Generalprobe
dress run – Hauptprobe
drive-in cinema – Autokino
drive motor – Antriebsmotor
drive on permission – Durchfahrgenehmigung
driver foreman – Leiter der Fahrbereitschaft
driving signal – Pilotsignal, Synchronsignal
drop-out – Aussetzfehler, Signalausfall
dry – trocken
dry cell – Trockenbatterie
drying box – Trockenschrank
drying mark – Trockenfleck
dry-mounting tissue – Trockenklebefolie
dry run – heiße Probe, Probedurchlauf
dual registration pin – Doppelsperrgreifer
dual role cast – Doppelgängerbesetzung
to dub – kopieren, synchronisieren
dubber – Bandspieler, Kopiermaschine
dubber for n tapes – Kopierstraße für n Bänder
dubbing – Synchronisation (aus einer Fremdsprache in die eigene Sprache)
dubbing actor – Synchronsprecher
dubbing in a foreign language – Synchronisation in eine Fremdsprache
dubbing loop – Synchronschleife
dubbing speaker – Synchronsprecher
dubbing theatre – Synchronstudio

to dub in – einblenden
to dub in (the) sound – einen Film mit Ton unterlegen
dull-finish paper, dull-surfaced paper – mattes Papier
duplicate positive – Dup-Positiv
duplicating negative – Duplikatnegativ
dup negative – Dup-Negativ
duration of developing – Entwicklungszeit
to dust – abstauben
dust cover – Staubschutz
dust particle – Staubkorn
dye – Farbstoff
dye coupling developer – Farbkupplungsentwickler
dye reducer – Farbabschwächer
dynamic characteristic – Röhrenkennlinie

E

to earn – einspielen
earphone – Kopfhörer
eccentric-in irising – exzentrische Aufblende
eccentric-out irising – exzentrische Abblende
echo chamber – Hallraum
echo picture – Doppelbild
echo plate – Hallplatte
edge light – Seitenlicht
edge number – Randnummern
edge of perforation – Perforationsseite
to edit – schneiden, montieren
edit controller – Schnittsteuerung
edit down – Umschnitt
edite suite – Schneideraum
editing – Filmschnitt, Montage, Schnitt
editing girl – Kleberin
editing list – Schnittliste
editing room – Schneideraum
editing table – Klebetisch, Schneidetisch
editor – Cutter, Cutterin, Redakteur
editor's assistant – Cutterassistent/in
edit suite (GB) – Schnittstudio, EB-Schneideraum
effective aperture – wirksame Öffnung, T-Blendenwert
effective area of antenna – wirksame Antennenfläche
effect lighting – Effektbeleuchtung
effects operator – Geräuschemacher
effect spot – Effektscheinwerfer
effects track – Geräuschband
efficiency – Wirkungsgrad
eighty six (*slang*) – abschalten
electret microphone – Elektretmikrofon
electrician – Elektriker
electric tension (voltage) – elektrische Spannung
electro acoustics – Elektroakustik
electromagnetic spectrum – elektromagnetisches Spektrum

electron gun – Elektronenkanone
electronic cut, electronic editing – elektronischer Schnitt
emergency generator – Notstromaggregat
emphasis – Anhebung, Hervorhebung, Betonung
emulsion – Emulsion
emulsion number – Emulsionsnummer
emulsion side – Schichtseite
emulsion speed – Filmempfindlichkeit
endboard – Schlußklappe
end credits, end titles – Abspann, Nachspann
energize – Speisung
enhancer – elektronischer Bildverbesserer
to enlarge – vergrößern
enlarger – Vergrößerer
entertainment tax – Vergnügungssteuer
envelope – Hüllkurve
equipment – Apparatur, Ausrüstung, Aufnahmeeinheit
to erase – löschen
erasing head – Löschkopf
established – eingeführt. Person oder Drehort, die bereits in einer Einstellung gezeigt wurde. Personen, die in »Spago's« Restaurant, Los Angeles, bekannt sind (*slang*)
establishing shot – Anfangseinstellung, gibt einen Überblick über die Szene
evening program – Abendprogramm
examining board – Prüfungsausschuß
exclusive rights – Ausschließlichkeitsrechte, Exklusivrechte
executive producer – Produktionsleiter
exhibition – Ausstellung
exhibition rights – Vorführrechte
exited phosphor – angeregter Leuchtstoff
exploitation of a film – Auswertung eines Films
exposition – Ausstellung
exposure – Belichtung
exposure control – Belichtungssteuerung
exposure counter – Bildzählwerk
exposure meter – Belichtungsmesser
exposure test – Belichtungsprobe
exposure time – Belichtungszeit

exposure tolerance – Belichtungsspielraum
exposure value – Lichtwert
extender – Brennweitenverdoppler
extension cord – Verlängerungskabel
extension tube – Zwischenring
extension view-finder – Sucherlupenverlängerung
exterior shot – Außenaufnahme
extra – Komparse, Requisite
extra vigorous – extrahart
eyelight – Augenlicht, Kopflicht
eye line – Blickrichtung von Schauspielern
eyepiece – Okular
eyepiece leveler – Sucherlupenhalterung

F

fade – optische Blende
fade in – Aufblende
fade out – Abblende
fader, fader unit – Ausblendschalter, Regler
false start – falscher Einsatz, falscher Start
Farmer's reducer – Farmerscher Abschwächer
fashion board – Titelkarton
fast film – hochempfindlicher Film
fast lens – lichtstarkes Objektiv
fast-motion – Zeitraffer
fast pulldown recorder – Schnellschaltwerk
to favor – eine Person hervorstellen
feature – Spielfilm
feature player – Hauptdarsteller
fee – Gage
feedback – Rückkopplung
feeding – Speisung
feeding claw – Transportgreifer
feed magazine – Abwickelkassette
feed reel – Abwickelrolle
feed side – Abwickelseite
female – Buchse
field impulse – V-Impuls, Vertikalimpuls
field of image – Bildfeld
field of view – Blickwinkel eines Kameraobjektivs
field pick-up – Außenreportage
field production – Außenproduktion
field sync signal, field synchronizing impulse – V-Impuls, Vertikalimpuls
field to frame synchronizer – Phasenschieber
file – Archivhülle
filler, fill-in light – Aufheller, Aufhellicht, Zusatzlicht
filler (US), fill-up film – Beifilm, Zwischenprogramm
fill-in transmitter – Füllsender, Umsetzer
to film – drehen
film archive – Archiv

Film Assesment Board – Filmbewertungsstelle
film-break – Filmriß
film career (GB) – Filmkarriere
film cartridge – Filmpatrone
film cement – Filmkitt, Kleber
film changing bag – Filmwechselsack
film cleaner – Filmreiniger
film clip – Filmklammer, Klammerteil
film course – Lehrfilm
film editor – Cutter, Cutterin
film equipment – Filmausrüstung
film feeding – Abwickelspule
film footage – Einblendmaterial
film frame – einzelnes Filmbild
film gate – Bildfenster
film gauges – Filmformat
filmgrader – Kopiermeister
film guide – Greifersystem
filmic, filmically – filmisch
film industry (GB) – Filmindustrie
filming – drehen, filmen
filming technique – Aufnahmeverfahren, Filmtechnik
film inspection – Kopienkontrolle
film jam – Filmsalat
film joiner – Klebelade, Klebepresse
film leader – Startband
film librarian – Filmarchivar
film loader – Materialassistent
film-maker – Filmschaffender
film music – Filmmusik
film on art – Kurzfilm
film on a vast scale – Monumentalfilm
filmpack back – Planfilmkassette
film processing station – Kopierwerk
film processing works – Kopierwerksarbeiten
film producer's indemnity insurance – Produktionsversicherung
film review – Filmbesprechung
film rights – Vervielfältigungsrechte von Filmen

film scanner – Filmabtaster, Filmgeber
film schedule – Aufnahmeplan
filmservice – Filmbüro
film-setting – Fotosatz
film shooting script – Drehbuch mit Details über jede Einstellung
film sound recorder – Lichttonkamera
film splicer – Klebelade, Klebepresse
film story – Handlung eines Film, Inhalt
film technicians – Filmschaffende
film transport system – Filmschaltwerk
film viewer – Laufbildbetrachter
film winder – Filmumroller, Umroller
filter – Filter
filter density – Filterdichte
filter factor – Verlängerungsfaktor
filter foil punch – Filterfolienstanze
filter holder – Filterhalter
filter wheel – Filterrad
final composite track – Endmischband
final cut – Endschnitt, Feinschnitt
final draft – Endfassung
final mix – Endmischung
final trial composite – Abnahmekopie
finder – Sucher
finder extender – Sucherlupenverlängerung
fine adjustment – Feineinstellung
fine-grain developer – Feinkornentwickler
fine graininess – Feinkörnigkeit
fine-grain master – Lavendelkopie
fine-grain print – Feinkornkopie für Trickfilme
fine-grain stock – Feinkornmaterial
fine tuning control – Feinregler
to finish – abdrehen
first answer print – Nullkopie
first assistant – Aufnahmeleiter
first broadcasting – Erstausstrahlung
first developer – Erstentwickler
first draft – erster Entwurf

first night, first run – Uraufführung
first release print – Vorführkopie
first trial color composite print – 1. Lichttonfarbkopie
first trial composite – 1. kombinierte Kopie
first unit – erste (Arbeits-) Schicht
fish eye lens – Fischaugenobjektiv
fishing rod, fishpole – Tonangel
fitting – Fassung, Zubehör
fixed angle – feste Bildeinstellung
fixed focal length lens – Festbrennweite
fixing salt – Fixiersalz
flack – Presseagent
flag – Blende, Lichtblende
flare – Überstrahlung
flash – Blitzlicht, Blitzlichtgerät, sehr kurzer Zwischenschnitt
flash-back – Rückblende
flash cube – Blitzlichtwürfel
flash frame – Einstellbild
flashgun – Blitzlicht
flash light photography – Blitzlichtaufnahmen
flash pan – Reißschwenk
flash-shoe – Blitzschuh
flash synchronization – Blitzsynchronisation
flatbed, flat bed editing machine – horizontaler Schneidetisch
flatbed view camera – Laufbodenkamera
flat film – Planfilm
flat print – normale, nicht anamorphotisch gepreßte Filmkopie
flat random noise – Röhrenrauschen
flesh tone – Gesichtsfarbe
flexible eyecup – faltbare Augenmuschel
flexible shaft – biegsame Welle
flick (*slang*), **flicker** (*slang*) – Film
floating elements – bewegliche Linsenglieder in Objektiven
flood lamp – Leuchte, Scheinwerfer
floor – Studio
floor level – Bodenhöhe
floor man – Bühnenarbeiter
floor manager – Aufnahmeleiter

florentine – Stufenlinsenscheinwerfer
fluff – Versprecher
to fluff – stottern, sich verhaspeln, sich versprechen
fluid drive – Hydroantrieb
fluid head – Hydrokopf
fluorescent tube – Leuchtstoffröhre
flyback trafo – Zeilenendtrafo
flying moon – Spezial HMI-Lampe (25kW), das bei einer amerikanischen Nacht Mondlicht simuliert
flying spot scanner – Lichtpunktabtaster
flywheel – Schwungmasse, Schwungrad
foam – Schaum
focal length – Brennweite
focal plane – Brennebene
focal plane shutter – Schlitzverschluß
focal point – Brennpunkt
focus – Schärfe
to focus – fokussieren, scharfstellen
focused at infinity – Unendlicheinstellung
focusing hood – Lichtschachtsucher
focusing range – Entfernungsbereich
focusing screen – Mattscheibe
focusing screen with central grid – Mattscheibe mit Mikroprismen
focusing screen with central grid and split-image range-finder – Mattscheibe mit Mikroprismen und Schnittbildentfernungsmesser
focusing screen with split-image range-finder – Mattscheibe mit Schnittbildentfernungsmesser
focus lever – Schärfenhebel
focus mark – Schärfemarkierung
focus operator, focus puller – Schärfeassistent
to focus up – Bild aus der Unschärfe in die Schärfe ziehen
fog – Nebel, Schleier
fog machine – Nebelmaschine
foil – Klebeband
folding camera – Klappkamera
fold-over – Doppelbild
follower – Verfolgungsscheinwerfer
follow focus mechanism – Schärfenzieheinrichtung

follow-pointer exposure meter – Nachführbelichtungsmesser
follow shot – Fahraufnahme, Verfolgungsaufnahme
follow spotlight, follow spot – Verfolgerlicht, Verfolgungsscheinwerfer
footage – Filmausschnitt, Muster
footage counter – Meter- (Fuß-)Zähler, Zählwerk
footage number – Fußnummern (Meternummer)
foot commutator – Fußschalter
foreground – Vordergrund
foreign correspondent – Auslandskorrespondent
foreign language operation – Synchronisation in eine fremdsprachige Version
foreign version of a film – fremdsprachliche Fassung eines Films
formalin fixer – Formalinfixierbad
forward action – Vorlauf, Vorwärtsgang
400 foot magazine – 120 m Kassette
fovea – blinder Fleck (Auge)
frame – Bild, einzelnes Filmbild, Vollbild
to frame – quadrieren, eine Einstellung einrichten, den Bildausschnitt festlegen
frame counter – Bildzähler
to frame down – den Bildstrich nach unten verstellen
frame gauge – Bildschritt
frame impulse – V-Impuls, Vertikalimpuls
frame jumps – Achsensprung
frame line – Bildstrich
frame scanning – Rasterabtastung
frames per second – Bildgeschwindigkeit, B/s, Bilder pro Sekunde
frame synchronizing impulse – V-Impuls, Vertikalimpuls
to frame up – den Bildstrich nach oben verstellen
frame view-finder – Rahmensucher
framing – bestimmen des Bildausschnitts, Bildstricheinstellung, Einrichten einer Einstellung
framing carriage – Bildstrichverstellung
framing control – Bildfangregler
framing mask – Bildmaske
framing oscillator – Bildablenkgenerator
freedom of press – Pressefreiheit
free-running – unverkoppelt

freeze effect – Stoptrick
freeze, freeze frame – Standbild, Standbildverlängerung
french flag – Lichtschutz, Neger (*slang*)
frequency response of recording – Aufnahmefrequenzgang
Fresnel lens spotlight – Stufenlinsenscheinwerfer
fresnel screen – Fresnelscheibe
friction pan-and-tilt head – Kugel-Schwenk- und Neigekopf
fringe area – Grenze des Sendegebietes, Empfangsgrenzgebiet
fringing – Unschärfe, Farbverlust
front credits – Filmvorspann
front glass – Frontlinse
front lens – Vorsatzlinse
front lens cap – vorderer Objektivdeckel
frontporch – Austastschulter
front standard – vordere Standarte
front standard assembly – Objektivträger
front view – Vorderansicht
frying – Zischen
full aperture film gate – Bildfenster im Stummfilmformat
full body – Planckscher Strahler, schwarzer Körper
full length film – Hauptfilm, abendfüllender Film
full modulation – Vollaussteuerung, Vollpegel, 100% Aussteuerung
full-scale deflection – Vollausschlag auf der Skala
full shot – Einstellung, die eine ganze Person zeigt
full track – Vollspur
fuse – Sicherung
fuzzy (*slang*) – unscharfes Bild

G

gadgets – Zusatzgerät
gaffer – Oberbeleuchter
gaffer grip, gaffer cramp – Krokodilklemme
gag-writer – Autor komischer Filmszenen
gain – Verstärkung
gain amplification – Vorverstärkung
gallery, gantry – Beleuchterbrücke
gamma – Steilheit, Gamma
gamma – Steilheit
gap – Spalt
gate pass – Durchfahrschein
gator grip (*slang*) – Krokodilklemme
gauze – Raster, Tüll
gear ring – Zahnkranz
general view – Übersicht
generating set – Stromaggregat
Geneva motion, Geneva movement – Malteserkreuzgetriebe
Geneva stop – Malteserkreuz
German version – deutsche Fassung
to get muddled – sich verhaspeln
to get up a part – eine Rolle einstudieren
ghost picture (GB) – Doppelbild
to give more voice – mehr Stimme geben
to give the lamps the juice (*slang*) – die Lampen einschalten
glass pane – Glasscheibe
glass perl screen – Perlleinwand
glass porcelain – Milchglas
glass shot – Trickaufnahme durch eine Glasscheibe, auf die fehlende Teile des Hintergrundes gemalt sind
glazed paper – Hochglanzpapier
globe – Glühlampe
glossary – Zusammenfassung
glossy – Hochglanzfoto
gobo – Neger (*slang*)
Goerz attachment – optische Bank

to go into production – Drehbeginn, die Produktionen beginnen
golden times (*slang*) – zuschlagpflichtige Sonn- und Feiertage
gradation – Gradation
graded neutral density filter – Grauverlauffilter
graded print (GB) – Korrekturkopie
grading – Filmempfindlichkeit, Lichtbestimmung
gradual filter, graduated filter – Verlauffilter
grain – Korn
grain density – Korndichte
graininess – Körnigkeit
grain size – Korngröße
gramophone amplifier – Schallplattenverstärker
grap-shot – Schnappschuß
graticle – Fadenkreuz
gray card – Aufsichtsgraukeil
grease-paint – Schminke
green – grün
grey scale – Graukeil, Stufenkeil
grid – Gitter
grid-clip – Klemme
grille – Konvergenztestbild
grip – Atelierarbeiter, für den Dolly, Kran und Kameraumbauten verantwortlich, Studioarbeiter; Schwenkgriff
grip-clip – Klemme
grip stand – Stativ
ground – Erdung, Masse
to ground – erden
ground cove – Hohlkehle
ground-glass disk, ground-glass screen – Mattscheibe
ground level – Bodenhöhe
groundrow – Rampenlicht
group fader (*slang*) – Summenregler
grub screw – Madenschraube
guidetrack – Primärton
gyro-tripod – Kreiselstativ

H

hackneyed – abgedroschen
hair – Fussel
hair-check – Fusselkontrolle
hair light – Spitze, Spitzlicht
half-apple box – Plattform mit halber Höhe
half scrim – halbe Drahtgaze
half-shade – Halbschatten
half silvered mirror – halbdurchlässiger Spiegel
half-sine wave – Halbwelle
halo – Lichthof
hand boom – Mikrofonangel
hand camera – Handkamera
hand-held lamp, hand-held light – Handlampe
hand rail – Schutzgeländer
to hang over – überhängen
hardener – Härtebad
hardener stop bath – Härtestopbad
hardening fixing bath – Härtefixierbad
hardening solution – Härtebad
hard focus – punktgenaues fokussieren
hard-front camera – Kamera mit einem Objektivbajonett anstatt eines Revolvers
»Hard Rock« – Spitzname für das Verwaltungsgebäude der ABC, New York
hard rubber – Hartgummi
hard shadow – Schlagschatten
haze filter – UV-Sperrfilter
hazy – unscharf
head – Filmanfang
head-and-shoulder portrait – Brustbild
head band – Kopfhörer
head bowl – Kugelschale
head electrician – Oberbeleuchter
headless screw – Madenschraube
headlines – Hauptrolle

head of department – Abteilungsleiter
head of publicity – Pressechef
heads alignment – Einmessen der Köpfe
headset – Kopfhörer-Mikrofon-Kombination
headset monitoring – Hinterbandkontrolle beim Tonbandgerät
head-support assembly – Kopfträger
head-to-tape pressure – Bandandruck
head wear – Kopfabrieb
heatable eyecup – heizbare Augenmuschel
heat-absorbing glass – Wärmeschutzfilter
heating drum – Trockentrommel
heavy current – Starkstrom
heavy shadow – Schlagschatten
height of picture – Bildhöhe
helicopter mount – Hubschrauberaufhängung
helix cable – Spiralkabel
high-angle shot – Vogelperspektive
high contrast – kontrastreich
high definition – hochauflösend, hochzeilig
high definition lens – Hartzeichner, hochauflösendes Objektiv
high-definition television – hochzeiliges Fernsehsystem
high frequency loudspeaker – Hochtonlautsprecher
high key – Beleuchtungstechnik mit geringem Kontrast
highlights – Lichter, Spitzlichter
high-photography – Vogelperspektive
high-piece – Sucherlupenverlängerung
high pitched sound – hoher Ton
high-pressure mercury lamp – Quecksilberhochdrucklampe
high resolution – hohe Auflösung
highroller – hohes Lampenstativ
high shot – Vogelschauperspektive
high-speed camera – Zeitlupenkamera
high-speed film – hochempfindlicher Film
high-speed objective – lichtstarkes Objektiv
high-stand – hohe Plattform
to hit the lights – die Lampen einschalten
hold frame – Standbildverlängerung
holding control – Bildfang

hold range – Synchronisationsbereich
hold take – gelungene Aufnahme
hologram – Hologramm
holography – Holografie
home movies – Heimkino
home technician – Kundendiensttechniker im Außendienst
homogeneous – monochromatisch
horizontal blanking – Zeilenaustastung
horizontal flyback – Zeilenrücklauf
horizontal frequency – Zeilenfrequenz
horizontal hold – Zeilenfangregler
horizontal image – Querbild
horizontal power – Zeilenfrequenz
horizontal retrace – Zeilenrücklauf
horizontal scan output transistor – Zeilenendstufentransistor
horizontal shift – Seitenverschiebung
horizontal size control – Bildbreitenregler
horizontal sweep – Zeilenablenkung
horizontal time-base generator – Zeilenkippgenerator
hot splicer – Heißklebepresse
hot spot – Überstrahlung auf dem Film
howl round – akustische Rückkopplung, Pfeiffen
hue – Farbton
hue-control – Farbwertregler
hue error – Farbabweichung
hum-free – brummfrei
humidity – Feuchtigkeit
hum voltage – Netzbrummfrequenz (50 Hz)
hunting disk – Abtastscheibe
hyphenate – Person, die in einem Film mehrere Funktionen hat, z. B. Produzent, Regisseur und Darsteller

iconoscope – Ikonoskop
identification leader – Allonge
idiot cards – Neger
idle current – Ruhestrom
illuminated frame finder – Leuchtrahmensucher
illumination – Beleuchtung
illumination level – Beleuchtungsstärke
image – Bild
image converter tube – Bildwandlerröhre
image defect – Abbildungsfehler
image diagonal – Bilddiagonale
image distance – Bildweite
image erecting prism – Umkehrprisma
image flickering – Bildflimmern
image frequency – Bilder pro Sekunde, Bildgeschwindigkeit, B/s, Bildwechselzahl
image interference – Bildstörung
image pattern (US) – Ladungsbild
image plane – Abbildungsebene
image point – Bildebene
image power amplifier – Bildendverstärker
image registration (US) – Rasterdeckung
image retaining panel – Bildspeicherplatte
image scale – Abbildungsmaßstab
image sensor – Bildwandler
image stabilizer – Bildstabilisator
image storing tube – Bildspeicherröhre
image transmission – Bildübertragung
image upside down – Kehrbild
impact sound – Trittschall
impact-sound filter – Trittschallfilter
in camera – im Blickfeld der Kamera
incandescent lamp – Glühlampe (Panlicht)
incidental advertising – Schleichwerbung
incident light meter – Luxmeter
to increase – erhöhen, zunehmen

incrustation – Filmabrieb
index – Inhaltsverzeichnis
index tube – Zebraröhre
indicator – Anzeigeinstrument
indicator gate – Hellsteuerimpuls
indoor shoot – Innenaufnahme
inductivity – Induktivität
infinity focusing, infinity focus – Unendlicheinstellung
information caption – Zwischentitel
infra-red – infrarot
infra-red image converter – Infrarotbildwandler
infra-red vidicon – Infrarotvidikon
in phase – phasengleich
input – Eingang
insert – Zwischenschnitt, Einblendung
insert car – Fahrzeug, das ein zu filmendes Fahrzeug (»target car«) zieht. Auf ihm sind Licht und Kamera montiert.
instantaneous shutter – Momentverschluß
instant print film – Sofortbildfilm
instant return mirror – Rückschwingspiegel
instruction book – Bedienungsanweisung
instruction manual – Handbuch
insulating layer – Sperrschicht
insurance take – Sicherheitseinstellung
intensity of current – Ampère, Stromstärke
inter carrier – Differenzträger
inter carrier sound system – Tonzwischenträgersystem
intercepting blade – Zwischenflügel einer Umlaufblende
interchangeable bellows – auswechselbarer Balgen
interchangeable finder system – auswechselbares Suchersystem
interchangeable groundglass frame – Rückteil-Wechselrahmen
interchangeable lens, interchangeable lens system – Wechselobjektiv
intercom – Interkom
intercut – Zwischenschnitt
inter dot flicker – Zwischenpunktflimmern
interlace – Zwischenspannung
interlaced field – Zeilensprung-Halbbild
interlaced scanning – Zeilensprung, Zeilensprungverfahren
interlock motor – Synchronmotor

intermediate blade – Zwischenflügel einer Umlaufblende
intermediate dup – Zwischenduplikat
intermediate frequency – Zwischenfrequenz
intermediate negative – Zwischennegativ
intermediate positive – Farbzwischenpositiv
intermediate standard – Hilfsstandarte
intermittent sprocket – Filmtransportrolle
intermodulation – Intermodulation
internal focusing – Innenfokussierung
internegative – Zwischennegativ
interpret – Darsteller
interval resistance – Innenwiderstand
interval signal – Pausenzeichen
in the can – abgedrehter Film
in the can – abgedrehter Film
inverse voltage – Sperrspannung
inverter – Gleichstrom auf Wechselstrom-Wandler
in working order – betriebsbereit
iris diaphragm – Irisblende
»It's a wrap!« – akzeptierte Aufnahme, »Gestorben!«

J

jack – Buchse
jamming – Rundfunkstörungen, die durch Störsender entstehen
jamming transmitter – Störsender
jelly – Gelatinefilter
jenny (*slang*) – Stromgenerator
jitter – Bildzittern, »Mäusezähnchen«-Effekt
joint transmitter – angeschlossener Sender
journalist – Journalist
juicer (*slang*) – Beleuchter, der die Lampen einschaltet
jump cut – Bildsprung durch einen Schnittfehler
junction – Sperrschicht
junior – 2kW Lampe
justiciary – Justitiar

K

»Keep off!« – »Eintritt verboten!«
key – Helligkeitsumfang, Helligkeitsgradation
keyboard – Tastatur
key grip – Studiovorarbeiter
key light – Führungslicht
key number – Randnummer
key stone – Trapezverzeichnung
kicker light – Aufheller
kick-light – Gegenlicht (innen), Spitze, Spitzlicht
to kill – abschalten
to kill a set – eine Dekoration abbauen
to kine – fazen
knob twister (*slang*) – Tonmann

L

lab, laboratory, laboratory for processing – Kopierwerk
laboratory lamp – Dunkelkammerlampe
lab report – Kopierwerksbericht
lacquering – Blankierung
to laminate – aufziehen, laminieren
lamp replacement – Lampenwechsel
landscape photography – Landschaftsfotografie
language dubbing – Nachsynchronisation in eine Fremdsprache
lanyard microphone – Lavaliermikrofon
lapel microphone – Anstecker, Ansteckmikrofon
large current – Starkstrom
large grain – grobkörnig
large size camera – Großformatkamera
latent – latent
lateral dollyshot – parallele Kamerafahrt, Parallelfahrt
lateral inversion – Seitenumkehr
laterally inverted image – seitenverkehrte Abbildung
latitude – Belichtungsspielraum
lavalier microphone – Lavaliermikrofon
lead – Hauptdarsteller
leader – Allonge, Startband, Vorspann
leader of the tape – Bandvorspann
leader tape – Vorspannband
leading actor – Hauptdarsteller
leading part – Titelrolle
leaf shutter – Zentralverschluß
leak current – Reststrom
leaking noise – Störgeräusch
left-to-right – von links nach rechts
legal adviser – Justitiar
legs (*slang*) – Stativ
lens – Objektiv
lens angle – Bildwinkel
lens-aperture – Objektivöffnung
lens axis – optische Achse

lensboard adapter – Objektivbühne bei Großformatkameras
lens coating – Linsenvergütung
lens element – Linsenglied
lens flange – Objektivhalter
lens for standard film camera – Normalfilmkamera-Objektiv
lens hood – Kompendium, Sonnenblende
lens mount – Objektivfassung
lens mounting ring – Objektivanschlußring
lens panel or lens standard – Objektivstandarte
lens plane – Objektivebene
lens pouch – Objektivbeutel
lens set – Satz von Objektiven
lens speed – Lichtstärke eines Objektivs
lens support – Objektivstütze
lens turret – Objektivrevolver, Revolverkopf
lenticulated film – Rasterfilm
level – Pegel
levelling – Nivellierschlitten
life model – Aktmodell
life transmission – Lifesendung
light – hell
light absorbing – Licht schluckend
light box – Lichtkasten
light dolly – Leichtdolly
light electrician – Beleuchter
lightening of a print – Abschwächung or Aufhellung einer Kopie
light filter – Lichtfilter
lighting – Beleuchtung
lighting equipment – Lichtausrüstung
lighting float – Lichtwanne
light leak – Lichteinfall
light meter – Belichtungsmesser
light platform – Beleuchterbrücke
light signal – Lichtsignal
light source – Lichtquelle
light struck – Lichteinfall
light trap – Lichtschleuse
lightweight matte box – Leichtkompendium

limelight – Rampenlicht
limit – Grenzwert, Spitzenwert
limiter – Begrenzer
line – Strippe (*slang*)
linearity – Linearität
line bend – Zeilenentzerrung
line blanking interval – Zeilenaustastlücke
line blanking pulse – Zeilenaustastimpuls
line control – Zeilensteuerung
line flicker – Zeilenflimmern
line-free – zeilenfrei
line frequency – Zeilenfrequenz, Zeilensprungverfahren
line hold – Zeilenfangregler
line interlace – Zeilensprungverfahren
line interlacing – Zeilensprung
line jitter – Zeilenspratzer
line-jump scanning – Zeilensprungverfahren
line lock – Zeilensynchronisation
line monitor – Kontrollmonitor
line of an actor – Rollenfach eines Schauspielers
line offset – Zeilenoffset
line output transformator, line output transformer – Zeilenablenktransformator
line pulling – Bildexpansion, Zeilenversatz, Zeilenwandern
line pulse – H-Impuls
line scan circuit – Zeilenkippschaltung
line scanning – Zeilenabtasten, zeilenweises Abtasten
line-scanning unit – Zeilenablenkeinheit
line-scanning voltage – Zeilenkippspannung
line shake – Zeilenflimmern
line slip – Zeilenschlupf
line spacing – Zeilenabstand
line standard – Zeilennorm
line structure – Rasterstruktur
line sync puls, line synchronisation impulse – H-Impuls, Zeilen-(synchronisations)impuls
line sync signal – Zeilengleichlaufsignal
line termination – Leitungsabschluß

line tilt – Zeilenentzerrung
to line up – einpegeln
line voltage fluctuation – Netzspannungsschwankung
line width – Zeilenbreite
lining-up – Motivsuche
lip microphone – Mikrofon für Nahbesprechung, Ansteckmikrofon, Anstecker
lip-sync – lippensynchron
liquid – flüssig
to listen – abhören
listening box – Monitorlautsprecher
living camera – entfesselte Kamera, Handkamera
load time – Röhrenkennlinie
to load, to load a camera – Film in eine Kamera einlegen, Film einlegen
locale, locality – Drehort, Schauplatz der Handlung
location – Drehort, Motiv
location shot – Außenaufnahme
location survey – Vorbesichtigung
lockdown knob – Verschlußhebel
locking – Synchronisation, Verkopplung
locking cam of the Geneva stop – Greifer
locking dark slide – Kassettenschieber
locking time – Hochlaufzeit, Synchronisationszeit, Verkopplungszeit
logbook – Schnittliste
log-sheet – Drehbericht, Negativbericht
long distance view – Fernaufnahme
long-focus – langbrennweitig
longitudinal scratch – Längsschramme
long shot – Aufnahme aus größerer Entfernung, Totale
long streaking – lange Fahnen, Farbschweife
long waves – Langwellen
loop – Schleife
loop projector – Schleifenprojektor
loop protector – Schleifenschutz
to loop the video signal – das Videosignal durchschleifen
loss of light – Lichtverlust
lot – Studioaußengelände
loudhailer (GB) – Lautsprecher

low-angle shot – Froschperspektive
low distortion – geringe Verzeichnung
low frequency – Niederfrequenz
low frequency noise – Zeilenrauschen
low key – Beleuchtungstechnik mit großem Kontrastumfang
low-light-level camera – Restlichtkamera
low-pass filter – Tiefbaßfilter
low sound – Baßton, tiefer Ton
low voltage halogen lamp – Niedervolthalogenlampe
luminescence – Lumineszenz
luminophor – Leuchtstoff
luminous arc – Lichtbogen
luminous sensitivity – Lichtempfindlichkeit
lunchroom (US) – Kantine

M

macbeth – Konversionsfilter, (Glühlicht auf Tageslicht)
macro switch – Makrohebel
magazine – Filmmagazin, Kassette
magazine arm – Spulenarm
magazine for polaroid film – Polaroidmagazin
magazine lid – Magazindeckel
magazine locking mechanism – Magazinverriegelung
magazine pouch – Kassettentasche
magazine slide – Magazinschieber
magenta – purpur
magic hour – Dämmerung
magnetic biasing – Vormagnetisierung
magnetic film – Cordband
magnetic laminating – Magnettonbespurung eines Films durch Aufkleben einer Randspur
magnetic recording medium – Magnettonmaterial
magnetic-striped film – Filmkopie mit Magnettonspur
magnetic striping – Magnettonbespurung eines Films durch Aufgießen einer Randspur
magnification – Vergrößerungsmaßstab
magnifier, magnifying glass – Lupe, Sucherlupe
main amplifier – Endverstärker, Hauptverstärker, Kraftverstärker, Leistungsverstärker
main reference library – Zentralarchiv
main switch – Hauptschalter
maintenance – Wartung
main title – Haupttitel, Vorspann
to make a statement of press – eine Presseerklärung abgeben
make-up – Schminke
to make-up – schminken
»Mark it!« – »Bitte die Klappe schlagen!« Anweisung an den Kameraassistent
married print – Filmkopie mit Lichttonspur
mask – Kasch, Maske, Vignette
masking plate – Rasterblende

master control board – Regiepult
master control room – Regieraum, Sendezentrale
master copy – Mutterband
master print – Musterkopien
master-recorder – Aufnahmerekorder
master shot – größte Totale in einer Sequenz
master sound track – Endmischband
master tape – Mutterband
master wing – Abdeckflügel einer Umlaufblende
matching – Farbabgleich, Farbkorrektur
matching format mask – Formatmaske
matching of a television aerial (antenna) cable – Abschluß des Fernsehkabels
material-defect – Materialfehler
mat paper – mattes Fotopapier
matte – Kasch, Vignette
matte box – Kompendium
matte shot – Aufnahme durch eine Maske
maximum aperture – Lichtstärke eines Objektivs
maximum level – Vollpegel
maximum rating – Grenzwert, Spitzenwert
maximum value – Maximalwert
meal period – Essenspause
mean value – Mittelwert
measuring range – Meßbereich
meat axe – Neger (*slang*)
mechanical shutter speed – mechanische Verschlußzeit
medium-format camera – Mittelformatkamera
medium long shot – Halbtotale
medium shot – Halbnaheinstellung
mega cycle – Megahertz
mercury lamp – Quecksilberlampe
merging curve – Hohlkehle
meter – Anzeigeinstrument
meter scale – Meterskala
metteur-en-scene (*slang*) – Realisator
microphone noise – Eigenrauschen von Mikrofonen
microphotography – Mikrofotografie

microscope adapter – Mikroskopadapter
micro strip – Mikrofilmstreifen
micro-tube – Mikrotubus
mid shot – Halbtotale, Halbnah
mike boom – Tonangel
minicam van – Ü-Wagen
minimum audible field – Hörschwelle
minimum brightness – Mindesthelligkeit
minimum focusing distance – Nahpunkt des Objektivs
mirror – Spiegel
mirror ball – Spiegelkugel
mirror lamp – Spiegellampe
miscast – Fehlbesetzung
mismatching – Fehlanpassung
»Missed the cue« – »Einsatz verpaßt!«
to mix – mischen, ansetzen
mixed feeds – Fremdquelleneinspeisung
mixed tracks – Mischband
mixer – Tonmann für die Tonmischung, Tonmischpult
mixing amplifier – Mischpultverstärker
mixing desk – Mischpult
mixing room – Tonstudio
mobile recording unit – Tonaufnahmewagen
mode – Betriebsart
model shot – Modellaufnahme
moderator (US) – Moderator
modulation – Modulation
modulation stage – Modulationstiefe
modulation transfer function – Modulationsübertragungsfunktion
Moiré effect – Moiré Effekt
moisture – Feuchtigkeit
monitor – Sichtgerät
monitor loudspeaker – Kontrollautsprecher
monitor picture – Vorschaubild
monitor room – Abhörraum, Ansichtsraum
monochrome camera – Schwarzweißkamera
monochrome monitor – Schwarzweißmonitor
monopod – Einbeinstativ

mono rail camera – optische Bankkamera
mono set (US) – Schwarzweißempfänger
mood – Stimmung
moo print – perfekte Filmkopie
motion-picture (US) – Film, Kinofilm
motion picture industry (US) – Filmindustrie
motor boating – Netzbrummen
motor pool – Fahrbereitschaft
to mount – Bilder aufziehen, Dias rahmen
movie – Film, Kino
movie career (US) – Filmkarriere
movie titler – Titelgerät
movie writer – Filmautor
moving adjusting pointer – Nachführzeiger
moving coil meter – Drehspulinstrument
moving coil microphone – Tauchspulmikrofon
moving matte – Overlay-Trickmischung
moving pin – Greiferantrieb
moving title – Wandertitel
multicoating – Mehrfachentspiegelung
multi-coupler – Antennenverstärker
multipath effect (US) – Doppelbild, Echobild, Geisterbild
multiple claw – Mehrfachgreifer
multiple exposure – Mehrfachbelichtung
multiplication factor – Verlängerungsfaktor
multi-range measuring instrument – Vielfachinstrument
mural – Hintergrundgemälde
music – Musik
musical director (GB) – Kapellmeister
musical leitmotif – musikalisches Thema
music and effects track – IT-Band, internationales Tonband
musicassette – Musikkassette
music editor – Schnittmeister für die Musik
music tape – Musikband
music track – Musikband
mute (GB) – stumme Filmkopie
mute shot – Filmaufnahme ohne Ton
mutilation of film – Filmbeschädigung
mystery play – Kriminalfilm

N

narration – Filmkommentar, Kommentar
narrator – Ansager, Rundfunksprecher
narrow gauge film – Schmalfilm (16mm)
near limit, near point – Nahpunkt
negative – Negativ
negative carrier – Filmbühne, Negativbühne
negative cutter – Negativabzieher, Negativabzieherin
negative cutting – Negativ abziehen
negative for archives purposes – Archivnegativ, eingelagertes Negativ
negative material – Aufnahmematerial
negative platform – Negativbühne
negative retouching – Negativretusche
negative stage – Negativbühne
negative with fine definition – fein durchgezeichnetes Negativ
nemo – Außenreportage
net feeding – Netzanschluß
net trouble – Netzstörung
network – Fernsehanstalt, Netzwerk
neutral grey – neutralgrau
neutral hue – neutraler Farbton
neutralizer – Neutralisierbad
neutral wire – Nulleiter
newcomer – Anfänger
newscast – Nachrichten
newscaster – Nachrichtensprecher
news flash – Kurzmeldung
newsmaster – Nachrichtensprecher
news material preparation – Anfertigung des Nachrichtenfilms
newspaper report – Pressebericht
news-reel – Wochenschau
Newton effect – Newtonscher Ring
night effect – amerikanische Nacht
night performance – Spätvorstellung
night premium – Nachtzuschlag
night shot – Nachtaufnahme

nitrate film, nitrate base film – Nitrofilm
noise – Rauschen
noise cancelling microphone – Mikrofon für Nahbesprechung
noise elimination, noise reduction – Rauschunterdrückung
nominal frequency – Nennfrequenz, Sollfrequenz, Sollgeschwindigkeit
non-conductor – Nichtleiter
non-fused earth – Schutzerde
non-linearity – Nichtlinearität
non-stop working time – durchgehende Arbeitszeit
non-synchron – asynchron
notation – Notiz
notching table – Stanztisch
n-power magnification – n-fach Vergrößerung
nude – Aktmodell
number of elements – Anzahl der Linsen
number of frames – Bildzahl

object distance – Objektweite
oblique projection – Schrägprojektion
oblique sound film splice – schräge Tonklebestelle
OB vehicle, OB van – Ü-Wagen
offcuts – Schnittmaterial
official presentation – öffentliche Vorführung
offset view-finder – Winkelsucher
Ohm's law – Ohmsches Gesetz
omega loop, omega wrap – Omega-Bandführung
on call – auf Abruf
on call – auf Abruf
one-light print – Einlichtkopie
one-to-one action – Einergang
one-way mirror – halbdurchlässiger Spiegel
on location – Außenaufnahme
opacity – Opazität
opening – Ausschnitt
opening credits – Vorspanntitel
opening music – Titelmusik
opening title – Vorspanntitel
operating cameraman – Kameramann, Schwenker
operating instructions – Bedienungsanleitung
optical – Trickblende
optical axis – optische Achse
optical bench camera – Großformatkamera
optical fibre – Glasfaserkabel
optical printing – optisches Kopieren
optical reduction – herunter kopieren, optische Verkleinerung
optical sound – Lichtton
orientable view-finder – Sucher mit automatischer Bildaufrichtung
original negative – Originalnegativ
original sound – O-Ton
original version – Originalfassung
originator – Urheber
orthicon – Orthikon

oscillation – Schwingung
outdoor location work – Außenaufnahmen
outfit – Aufnahmeeinheit, Ausrüstung
outgoing signal – Studioausgangsbild
outlet – Steckdose
outline – Umriß
out of frame – außerhalb des Blickwinkels der Kamera, nicht im Bildfeld
out of rack – verschobener Bildstrich im Filmprojektor
out of sync – asynchron
output – Ausgang
output level – Ausgangsspannung
outside broadcast – Außenreportage, Außenübertragung
outside diameter of lens mount – Außendurchmesser des Objektivanschlußes
out-takes – Schnittreste
over-all lighting – Grundlicht
overdevelopded negative – überentwickeltes Negativ
over developing, over-development – Überentwicklung
to overexpose – überbelichten
over-exposure – Überbelichtung
overfootage – Überlänge
overhead lighting – Oberlicht
overhead projector – Tageslichtprojektor
overhead shot – Einstellung von oben
overlay – Overlay-Trickmischung
overlength – Überlänge
overmodulation – Übersteuerung
to overrun – die Sendezeit überziehen
to overseam – überschreiben
overshoot – Überschwinger
overvoltage – Überspannung
owners manual – Bedienungsanweisung

P

paint – Schminke
paint pots – Farbwertregler
to pan – schwenken (horizontal)
panaclear – Regenabweiser
pan-and-tilt head – Schwenkkopf
pancake – Bühnenkiste
panchromatic – panchromatisch
panchromatic stock – panchromatischer Schwarzweißfilm
pan glas – Kontrastglas
panhandle – Schwenkarm
panning – Kameraschwenkung
panning handle – Schwenkarm
panning shot, pan shot – Panoramaschwenk
panorama head – Panoramakopf, Panoramaschwenkkopf
panorame – Weitwinkelaufnahme
panoramic screen – Panoramaleinwand
panoramic shot – Panoramaaufnahme
panpot – Panoramaregler
paper-to-paper – Klammerteil
parabolic antenna – Parabolantenne
parabolic mirror – Parabolspiegel
parallax – Parallaxe
parallel (US) – Praktikabel
parallel connection – Parallelschaltung
parasitic noise level – Störpegel
parochial cinema – Pfarrkino
partial exposure – Teilbelichtung
partial mask – Teilmaske
party line – Interkom
passepartout – Passepartout
patch bay, patchboard, patch panel – Steckfeld
patron – Zuschauer
pattern distortion – Ablenkfehler
pay-TV – Abonenntenfernsehen
PC spot – Stufenlinsenscheinwerfer

pea bulb – Startmarkierungslampe
peak indicator – Spitzenwertmesser
peak limiter – Amplitudenbegrenzer
peak of sound – Tonhöhe
peak value – Grenzwert, Spitzenwert
pearl screen – Perlleinwand
pedestal – (fahrbares) Studiostativ; Schwarzwert
to pep up – aufmöbeln
per diem – Spesen
perforated magnetic film – Cordband
perforation – Perforation
perforation gauge – Perforationsschritt
perforation hole – Perforationsloch
performance – Vorstellung
period costume – zeitgenössisches Kostüm
period music – zeitgenössische Musik
periscopic lens attachment – periskopischer Kameravorsatz
periwig – Perücke
perpendicular view – Senkrechtaufnahme
persistence – Nachleuchten
persistence of vision – Augenträgheit, Nachleuchteffekt
personal microphone – Anstecker, Ansteckmikrofon, Lavaliermikrofon
phantom powered microphone – phantomgespeistes Mikrofon
phase – Phasenlage, Trickfilmphase
phase angle – Phasenwinkel
phase change – Phasenänderung
phase condition – Phasenbedingung
phase difference – Phasendifferenz
phase response – Phasengang
phase shift – Phasenänderung
phase shifter – Phasenschieber
phase synchronisation – Regelspannungssynchronisation
phase voltage – Phasenspannung
phosphorescence – Nachleuchten, Phosphoreszenz
photo album – Fotoalbum
photocell blocking layer – Sperrschichtzelle
photo chemicals – Fotochemikalien
photo-composition – Fotosatz

photo-conducting camera tube – C-MOS Chip
photo-conductor – Fotowiderstand
photocopier, photocopying apparatus – Fotokopiergerät
photo dealer – Fotohändler
photoelectric cell – Fotoelement, Fotozelle, Fotodiode
photoelectric noise level – Rauschanteil
photogenic – fotogen
photogrammetry – Fotogrammetrie
photographer – Fotograf
photographic dark room – Dunkelkammer
photographic grade chemicals – fotografische Chemikalien
photographic laboratory – Fotolabor
photographic paper – Fotopapier
photo library – Bildarchiv
photometer – Belichtungsmesser
photometric steptype wedge – Stufenkeil
photometry – Photometrie
photosetting – Fotosatz
pick-up – Schnittbild, Zwischenschnitt, Tonabnehmer
pick-up equipment – Aufnahmeeinheit
pick-up head – Hörkopf
pick-up tube – Aufnahmeröhre, Bildröhre
pick-up velocity – Abtastgeschwindigkeit
picture – Bild, Film, Vollbild
picture and waveform monitor – Bildkontrollgerät, Kontrolloszilloskop
picture angle – Bildwinkel
picture area – Bildfeld
picture black – Schwarzpegel
picture carrier – Bildträger
picture change over – Bildüberblendung
picture control – Bildaussteuerung
picture daily print – Klatsche (*slang*), Positivbildmuster
picture definition – Auflösung
picture dup-negative – Negativ-Bild-Dup
picture editing – Bildschnitt
picture element – Bildpunkt
picture gamma – Bildgamma
picture gate – Bildfenster

picture geometry fault – Bildfehler
picture halftone – Grauwert
picture information – Bildinformation
picture join – Ausgleich der Geschwindigkeitsdifferenz zwischen Film und Fernsehbildern
picture negative report – Negativbericht
picture noise – Bildrauschen
picture point – Bildpunkt
picture quality – Bildqualität
picture ratio – Bild-Seitenverhältnis
picture repetition frequency – Bildfolgefrequenz
picture scan – Bildablenkung
picture scanning – Bildabtastung
picture signal – Bildsignal, Videosignal
picture size – Bildformat
picture slip – Bilddurchlauf
picture steadiness – Bildstand
picture superimposition (GB) – Rasterdeckung
picture sync pulse – Bildgleichlaufimpulse
picture tone – Trägerfrequenz
picture white – Weißpegel, Weißwert
picture window – Bildfenster
piezoelectricity – Piezoelektrizität
piezoelectric microphone – Kristallmikrofon
pilot frequency – Pilotton
pilot frequency recording – Pilottonverfahren
pilot lamp – Kontrollampe
pilot pins – Sperrgreifer
pilot program – Versuchssendung
pincer – Pinza
pincushion distortion – kissenförmige Verzeichnung
pinhole – Sperrgreifer
pin movement – Greiferbewegung
pin rack – Filmgalgen
pipe grid – Rohrgitter
pirated film – Raubkopie
pistolgrip – Pistolengriff
pitch – Tonfrequenz, Tonhöhe
pitch control – Regelung der Zeilenzahl

pitch of sound – Tonhöhe
pitch variation – Tonhöhenschwankungen
pivoting view-finder – schwenkbare Sucherlupe
pixel – Bildelement
plain glass screen – Klarglasscheibe
plane-convex lens – Plankonvexlinse
plane mirror – Planspiegel
plano-concave – plankonkav
plano-convex spotlight – Stufenlinsenscheinwerfer
plasticity – Raumwirkung des Bildes
platen – Andruckglasscheibe
plate voltage – Anodenspannung
playback amplifier – Wiedergabeverstärker
playback head – Hörkopf, Wiedergabekopf
playback loss – Abspielfehler
playback process – Rückspielverfahren
plot – Inhaltsangabe
plotting scale – Maßstab
plug – Schleichwerbung, Stecker
pocket ident – Zahlenfächer
pointer – Zeiger
point image – punktförmige Abbildung
point of view – subjektive Kamera, Substituierung, Standpunkt
point-of-view shot – Austausch, Substitution eines Darstellers
polarization filter – Polfilter
polarized lens – Objektiv mit vorgesetztem Polfilter
polarizing spectacles – Polarisationsbrille
pola screen – Polarisationsfilter
polishing – blankieren
to polish out – eine Filmkopie putzen
pool-hall lighting – Beleuchtung mit nur einer Deckenlampe, die im Bild sichtbar ist
portable camera – Handkamera
position of microphone – Mikrofonaufstellung
positive amplitude modulation – positive Amplituden modulation
positive print – Umkehrfilm
post-dubbing – Nachsynchronisation
post production – Film- und Videonachbearbeitung
to postsynchronize – Nachsynchronisieren

post-sync loop – Synchronschleife
to pot – den Ton aussteuern
potentiometer – Potentiometer
powder – Pulver, pulverförmig
power amplification – Leistungsverstärkung
power amplifier – Endverstärker, Hauptverstärker
power consumption – Leistungsaufnahme
powering unit – Speisemodul
power pack – Akku
power supply – Netzanschluß, Speisung, Stromversorgung
power zoom – Zoomobjektiv mit elektrischem Antrieb
practicable – Praktikabel
practical lamp – Lampe, die sichtbar in der Dekoration steht
pre-amplifier – Vorverstärker
to pre-assemble – vorbauen
pre-assembly shop – Vorbaubühne
pre-assembly studio – Vorbauhalle
pre-discharge – Restentladung
preflash, prefof – diffuse Vorbelichtung
pre-for listening – Vorhören
pre-hardener – Vorhärtebad
pre-magnetising – Vormagnetisierung
premier – Uraufführung
pre-mix, pre-mixing – Vormischung
preparation of news material – Anfertigung eines Nachrichtenfilms
preroll time – Hochlaufzeit, Startvorlaufzeit
pre-school broadcasting – Vorschulprogramm
pre-scoring – Tonaufnahme, bevor das Bild aufgenommen wird
to present – moderieren, herausbringen
presenter – Moderator
presenting editor – Studioredakteur
preservative – Schutzbeschichtung
preset – Voreinstellung
pre-setting studio – Vorbauhalle
press – Presse
press agency – Presseagentur
press agent – Presseagent
press card – Presseausweis
press commentary, press release – Pressekommentar

press conference – Presseempfang, Pressekonferenz
pressing roller – Andruckrolle
press law – Pressegesetz
press release – Pressebericht, Pressemeldung
press review – Pressestimmen
pressure gate – Andruckfenster
pressure pad – Andruckkufe
pressure plate – Andruckplatte
pressure-sensitive laminator – Kaltlaminiergerät
preview monitor – Vorschaumonitor
primaries – Primärvalenzen
primary colors – Grundfarben
prime lens – Festbrennweite, festbrennweitiges Objektiv
prime time – Hauptsendezeit
principal axis – optische Achse
print – Abzug, Kopie
printer fade – Kopierwerksblende
printer light – Kopierlicht
print film – Kopierfilm
to print in – einkopieren
printing length – Kopierlänge
printing light – Kopierlicht
printing loss – Kopierverlust
printing machine – Kopiermaschine
printing process – Kopierverfahren
»Print it!« – »K.«, »Kopierer«, Bemerkung im Negativbericht
print positive – Positivfilm
print stock – Kopierfilmmaterial
print-through – Übersprechen (durchkopieren) bei gewickeltem Magnetfilm
prism – Prisma
prismatic lens, prism lens – Prismenfilter
prism view-finder – Prismensucher
private performance – geschlossene Vorstellung
to process – verarbeiten
processing – Entwicklung
processing step – Arbeitsphase, Arbeitsschritt
processor – Entwicklungsmaschine
producer – Produktionsleiter, Produzent

production – Produktion
production assistant – Produktionsassistent
production budget – Produktionsetat
production company – Produktionsfirma
production consumables – Verbrauchsmaterial
production cost – Herstellungskosten, Produktionskosten
production credits – Vor- oder Nachspann, Titel
production designer – künstlerischer Gestalter
production director – Sendeleiter
production list – Stabliste
production manager – Aufnahmeleiter, Produktionsleiter, Sendeleiter
production matte box – Produktionskompendium
production number – Produktionsnummer
production planning department – Zentraldisposition
production recording channel – Aufnahmekanal
production schedule – Produktionsplan
production secretary – Produktionssekretärin
product placement – Schleichwerbung
program offer – Programmangebot
progressive interlace – Zeilensprungverfahren
to project – vorführen
projection – Projektion, Vorführung
projectionist – Vorführer
projection lenses – Projektionsobjektiv
projector – Projektor
projetion angle – Projektionswinkel
projetion booth – Vorführkabine
projetion distance – Projektionsentfernung
projetion gate – Projektionsfenster
projetion machine – Projektor
projetion permit – Vorführgenehmigung
projetion screen – Projektionswand
prologue – Vorprogramm
prolongation factor – Verlängerungsfaktor
prompter – Prompter, Textgeber, Textprojektor
propaganda film – Propagandafilm
property department – Atelierfundus, Fundus
property man, property master – Requisiteur
prop maker – Ausstatter für spezielle Requisiten

props – Dekorationsmaterial
protecting coat – Schutzschicht
protective ground – Schutzerde
provisional title – Arbeitstitel, vorläufiger Titel
pseudosolarisation – Pseudosolarisation, Sabattier-Effekt
public domain material – Film, der ohne Zahlung von Lizenzgebühren gesendet werden kann
publicity – Anzeige, Reklame, Veröffentlichung
publicity manager – Pressechef
pull down claw – Transportgreifer
to pull focus – Schärfe ziehen
pulse – Impulse
pup – 1/2kW Lampe, Pinza
pupil – Pupille
puppet film – Puppenfilm
push-pull amplifier – Gegentaktverstärker
to put in the library – archivieren
to put on 1.000Hz – 1.000Hz-Ton aufschalten
to put out – Agenturmeldung absetzen

Q

quality of reproduction – Wiedergabequalität
quality of sound, quality of tone – Tonqualität
quarter track – Viertelspur
quarz-light – Halogenlicht
1/4 inch tape – Senkelband, 1/4 Zoll Tonband
quick change magazine – Schnellwechselkassette
quick-focusing handle – Fokussiergriff
quick forward action – schneller Vorlauf
quick motion – Zeitraffer
quick reverse, quick reverse action – schneller Rücklauf

R

rabbit ears (*slang*) – Zimmerantenne
to rack focus – die Schärfe nachziehen
rack line – Bildsteg
rack processing – Rahmenentwicklung
radiant sensitivity of a camera tube – Empfindlichkeit der Aufnahmeröhre
radiation – Strahlung
radio frequency – Hochfrequenz
radio mast – Antennenmast
radio microphone – drahtloses Mikrofon, Funkmikrofon
radio OB – Hörfunkreportage, Ü-Wagen
radio telephone – Funksprechgerät
radius of curvature – Krümmungsradius
radius of the service area – Sendegebiet
rails – Schiene
rainbow wheel – Farbenrad
rain cover – Regenschutz, Wetterschutzhaube
raincover – Regenschutz
rain of a film – verkratzter Film
range extender – Brennweitenverdoppler
range-finder – Entfernungsmesser
range of adaptilities – Anwendungsbereich
range of contrast – Kontrastumfang
range of reception – Empfangsbereich, Sendegebiet
rapid developer – Rapidentwickler
rapid fixer – Schnellfixierbad
rapid-winding crank – Schnelltransportkurbel
raster scan – zeilenweises Abtasten
rated power output – Nennleistung
rating – Feststellen der Zuschauerzahlen, Sehbeteiligung
ratio – Verhältnis
raw stock (US) – Rohfilmmaterial, unbelichtetes Filmmaterial
raw stock manufacture – Rohfilmhersteller
ray of light – Lichtstrahl
reaction shot – Gegenschuß
reader – Lektor

reading error – Lesefehler
reading time – Lesebereich
realization of a feature – Inszenierung eines Films
rear lens cap – hinterer Objektivdeckel
rear surface – letzte Linse
rear view – Rückansicht
receiver – Empfänger
receiver licence fee – Rundfunkgebühr
record – Tonaufnahme, Schallplatte
recording amplifier – Aufnahmeverstärker
recording conditions – Aufnahmebedingung
recording current – Aufsprechstrom
recording head – Sprechkopf
recording of the commentary – Sprachaufnahme
recording system – Aufnahmesystem
recordist – Tonmann
record office – Tonarchiv
record-reproduce amplifier – Aufnahme-Wiedergabeverstärker
rectangular sunshade – Rechtecksonnenblende
rectification of frequency modulation – FM-Demodulation
recuperation of the silver – Silberrückgewinnung
red – Rot
re-development – Nachentwicklung, Verstärkung
to redress – entzerren (beim Vergrößern)
to re-dress – Szenenumbau
reducer – Abschwächer
reducing adapter – Reduzieradapter
reduction – Verkleinerung
reduction cassette – Reduzierkassette
reduction print – Verkleinerungskopie
to re-edit – umschneiden
re-editing – Feinschnitt
reel – Entwicklungsspirale, Spule, Spulenarm
reel-to-reel recorder – Spulentonbandgerät
re-exposure – Zweitbelichtung
reference pattern – Vergleichsbild
reference tape – Bezugsband
reflection densitometer – Auflichtdensitometer

reflection factor – Reflexionsfaktor
reflection losses – Reflextionsverlust
reflector – Reflektor, Scheinwerfer, Silberblende
reflector direction – Licht setzen, Scheinwerferführung
to reflect out – ausspiegeln
reflex camera – Spiegelreflexkamera
reflex view-finder – Reflexsucher
to refocus – Bild aus der Unschärfe ziehen
to regenerate – regenerieren
regeneration of film – Regenerierung eines Filmes
register pin, registration pin – Sperrgreifer
rehearsal screen test – Probeaufnahme
reissue – Reprise
relative aperture – Öffnungsverhältnis, relative Öffnung
relay – Relais
relay optics – optisches Relaissystem
release – Auslöser
release print – Massenkopie, Serienkopie, Verleihkopie, Vorführkopie
to re-light – eine Szene neu einleuchten
to remain – verbleiben
remake – Neuinszenierung eines alten Films, Neuverfilmung, Neuproduktion, Wiederverfilmung
remote cable switch – elektrische Fernbedienung
remote control – Fernbedienung, Fernschaltung
remote switch cable – Fernauslösekabel
remote tuning device – Fernbedienung
replenisher – Nachfüllösung, Regenerator
report film – Reportagefilm
report sheet – Drehbericht, Negativbericht
reproducing level – Abhörpegel
reproducing loss – Abspielfehler
reproduction – Wiedergabe
to re-record – umspielen, umspielen
re-recorded reel – Mischband
re-recording – Mischung, Überspielung
re-release – Wiederaufnahme eines Films ins Kinoprogramm
re-run – Wiederholung eines Films im Fernsehprogramm
residual charge – Restladung

resolution – Auflösung
resolving power – Auflösungsvermögen
resonance curve – Resonanzkurve
resonance peak – Resonanzspitze
to respool – umrollen, umspulen
retained image – Nachbild
retake (US) – Wiederholung einer Aufnahme, Wiederholungsaufnahme
reticle – Fadenkreuz
reticulation – Runzelkorn
to retouch – retuschieren
retouching dye – Retuschierfarbe
retouching pencil – Retuschierpinsel
return wire – Nulleiter, Rückleiter
revenues – Einnahmen
reverberant – hallig
reverberation plate – Hallplatte
reverberation time – Nachhallzeit
reversal exposure – Umkehrbelichtung
reversal film – Umkehrfilm
reverse action – Rücklauf
reverse angle, reverse shot – Gegenschuß
reverse voltage – Sperrspannung
review – Kritik
reviewer – Kritiker
revised draft – überarbeitete Fassung
to rewind – umrollen
rewinder – Umroller
re-write – Überarbeitung
to re-write – Überarbeiten
rheostat resistor – Widerstand (als elektronisches Bauteil)
to ride the focus – die Schärfe ziehen
to ride the gain, to ride the needle, to ride the spot – Überprüfen des Signals mit Messgeräten
to rig – aufstellen
rigging – Beleuchterbrücke
rigging tender – Rüstwagen
rights – Rechte
rights per release print – Rechte an einer Kopie

right-to-left – von rechts nach links
to rig the lamps – die Lampen aufbauen
rim-light – Gegenlicht (innen), Spitze, Spitzlicht
to rinse – ausspülen, wässern
rinsing – Wässerung
to rip and read – Verlesen von Nachrichten, sobald sie aus dem Telex kommen
riser – Praktikabel
ritter – Windmaschine
road show – Film, der nur in den großen Kinos läuft
roll film – Rollfilm
rolling shot – Aufnahme aus dem Auto
rolling title – Rolltitel
rolling tripod – Fahrstativ
roll number – Rollennummer
to roll-off – Beschneiden der tiefen und hohen Frequenzen mit Filtern
roll-off filter – Filter, daß die tiefen und hohen Frequenzen beschneidet
»Roll!«, »Roll camera!«, »Roll'em!« – »Film ab!«, Anweisung an den Kameramann
»Roll sound!« – »Ton ab!«, Anweisung an den Tonmeister
roof prism – Dachkantprisma
room acoustics – akustische Raumgestaltung, Raumakustik
room noise, room sound, room tone – Atmo, Raumatmosphäre, Raumatmo
rostrum – Tribüne, Praktikabel
rostrum bench – Tricktisch
rotary action – Drehbewegung
rotary shutter – Umlaufblende
rotary slide magazine – Rundmagazin
rotating floor – Drehbühne
rough cut – Rohschnitt
rough treatment – Rohdrehbuch
roundy round – 180° Schwenk der Kamera
royalties – Tantiemen
R-rated (US) – Film, der für Jugendliche unter 16 Jahre freigegeben ist, wenn sie von einem Erwachsenen begleitet werden
rubber spider – Gummispinne
rumble – Rumpelgeräusch
rumble pot – Topf mit Kunsteis, um Nebel zu erzeugen

run – Auflage, Ausstrahlung eines Programms, Lauflänge eines Films
run-by – Vorbeifahrt
run-down – Sendefolge
»Running!« – »Läuft!«
running – Ausstrahlung eines Films
running gag – roter Faden
running order – Ablaufplan
running shot – Gang mit der Handkamera
running speed – Filmlaufgeschwindigkeit
running time – Lauflänge, Laufzeit, Spielzeit eines Films, Vorführdauer
running water – fließendes Wasser
run-through – Probe mit abgeschalteten Kameras, Probedurchlauf, Stellprobe
to run through – eine Szene durchspielen
run-up time – Hochlaufzeit
rupture in characteristic curve – Kennlinienknick
rush (GB), rushes (GB), rush print (GB) – AK, Arbeitskopie, Bildmuster, Klatsche (*slang*), Muster

S/N ratio – Dynamik, Dynamikbereich, Störabstand
safebase film – Sicherheitsfilm
safelight – Dunkelkammerbeleuchtung
safe title area – Titelkasch
safety film – Sicherheitsfilm
salary – Gage, Honorar
sampling frequency – Schaltfrequenz
sandbag – Bühnengewicht
saturation – Sättigung
»Save it!« – »Kopieren!« Anweisung an das Scriptgirl
»Save the arcs!«, »Save the lights« – »Licht aus!«, Anweisung an den Beleuchter
to save the lights – die Beleuchtung ausschalten
scaffolding – Beleuchterbrücke
scale of reproduction – Vergrößerungsmaßstab
to scan – abtasten
scanner – Filmgeber, Filmabtaster
scanning – Abtastung, Beschreibung
scanning beam – Abtaststrahl, abtastender Elektronenstrahl
scanning component – Ablenkeinheit
scanning device – Abtastgerät
scanning gap – Abtastspalt
scanning spots of a line – Zeileninhalt
scan ring – Zeileneinschwinger
scar – Schramme
scenario – Buch, Drehbuch
scenario editor – Chefdramaturg
scenarist – Drehbuchautor
scene – Szene
scene of action – Schauplatz der Handlung, Drehort
scene of shooting – Drehort
scenery – Hintergrund (sowohl natürlicher bei Außenaufnahmen als auch künstlicher bei Studioaufnahmen), Szenenbild
scenery – Bühnenbild, Dekoration
scene slate – Filmklappe, Synchronklappe

scenic artist – Prospektmaler
schedule – Terminplan
schedule of features – Spielplan
Scheimpflug adjustment – Verschwenkung nach Scheimpflug
school broadcasting, school radio – Schulfunk
score – Filmmusik
Scotchlite process – Frontprojektionsverfahren mit einer Scotchlite Leinwand
scraper – Filmhobel, Retouchiermesser, Schabemesser
scratch – Bildschramme, Kratzer, Schramme
scratch track – Ton-Arbeitskopie
screen – Leinwand
to screen – verfilmen
screen grid – Schirmgitter
screen height – Bildwandhöhe
screening can – Abschirmkappe
screening of the rushes – Mustervorführung
screening room – Vorführraum
screen mask – Bildwandabdeckung
screenplay – Drehbuch
screenrights – Verfilmungsrecht
screen voltage – Schirmgitterspannung
screenwriter – Drehbuchautor
scrim – Drahtgaze, Gazeschirm, Softscheibe
script – Buch, Drehbuch
script clerk, script girl – Scriptgirl
scripter, script-writer – Texter
sealing tape – Klebeband
second answer print – zweite Korrekturkopie
secondary action – Nebenhandlung
secondary coil – Sekundärwicklung
secondary image – Nebenbild
second showing – Zweitausstrahlung
second unit – zweites Team
sectional view – Schnittbilder
security regulations – Sicherheitsvorschriften
segue – Überleitung von einer Szene zur anderen
to select – auswählen

selenium cell – Selenzelle
self-keyed insertion – Overlay-Trickmischung
self timer – Selbstauslöser
semi-automatic diaphragm – Spingblende
semi close-up – Halbnah
semiconductor – Halbleiter
senior – 5kW Stufenlinse
sensitive – empfindlich
sensitive to light – lichtempfindlich
sensitometer – Sensitometer
sensitometry – Sensitometrie
sentizing – Sensibilisierung
seque – Tonüberblendung
sequential scanning – zeilenweises abtasten
service area – Empfangsbereich, Sendegebiet
servo-lock time – Servo-Hochlaufzeit, Verkopplungszeit, Synchronisationszeit
servo motor – Selbstregelmotor
servo zoom drive – Zoom Antrieb
set – Atelier, Bühne, Dekoration, Drehort, Kamerastandort, Motiv, Requisite, Studio, Szenenbild
to set – Schauspielern und Kamera nehmen die Ausgangsposition ein
to set a hair light – eine Spitze setzen
set brake – Drehpause
set decoration by ... – Ausstattung von ...
set decorator – Ausstatter, Requisiteur
set dresser – Bühnenarbeiter
set of lenses – Objektivsatz
set of wires – Kabelsalat
set secretary (US) – Produktionssekretärin
to set the stop – die Blende einstellen, abblenden
setting – Szenenbild
setting angle – Einstellwinkel
setting of a feature – Filmbauten
setting of the lamps – Einleuchten
to set up a shot – eine Szene einrichten
to set up the camera – die Kamera einstellen
shade – Nuance, Färbung, Schattierung

shader – Bildingenieur, Kontrastregler
shadow – Schatten
shadow detail – Schattendurchzeichnung
shadow mask tube – Masken-Farbbildröhre, Maskenbildröhre
shadow scratch – Schramme
shallow depth, shallow focus – Tiefenschärfe
sharpness – Schärfe
sheet film – Planfilm
sheet film holder – Planfilmkassette
shielded cable – abgeschirmtes Kabel
shipping department – Versandabteilung
to shoot – eine Aufnahme wiederholen, nachdrehen
shooting angle – Aufnahmewinkel, Aufnahmebildwinkel
shooting break – Drehpause
shooting day – Drehtag
shooting distance – Aufnahmeentfernung
shooting field – Aufnahmefeld
shooting pattern, shooting plan – Drehplan
shooting range – Aufnahmeentfernung
shooting ratio – Drehverhältnis
shooting schedule – Aufnahmeplan, Drehplan
shooting script – Buch, Drehbuch
shooting studio – Atelier, Studio
shooting the playback – Drehen mit Playback Ton
shoot-off – Einstellung, bei der die Kamera hinter die Kulissen der Dekoration sieht
to shoot with low speed – unterdrehen, Zeitraffer
short circuit – Kurzschluß
short-distance shot – Nahaufnahme
short end – unbelichteter Filmrest
short film, short – Kurzfilm
shot – Aufnahme
shotgun – Kanone (*slang*), Richtmikrofon
shot sheet – Liste der Einstellungen für den E-Schwenker
shoulder pod – Schulterstativ
shoulder strap – Trageriemen
show print – Vorführkopie
shrinkage, shrinkage of the film – Schrumpfung, Filmschrumpfung

shutter – Umlaufblende, Verschluß
shutter control – variable Sektorenblende
shutter release – Drahtauslöser
shutter time – Verschlußzeit
sibilants – Zischlaut
side car mount – Autostativ
side-cutting plier – Seitenschneider
side light – Seitenlicht
side lighting – Seitenbeleuchtung
side of celluloid – Blankseite
side of coating – Schichtseite
signal – Nutzton
signal distortion – Signalverzerrung
signal level – Signalstärke
signalling clock – Signaluhr
silent movie – Stummfilm
silent speed – Synchrongeschwindigkeit (24, 25 or 30B/s)
silk – Seidenblende
silver halide – Halogensilber
silver recovery – Silberrückgewinnung
simplex microphone – phantomgespeistes Mikrofon
single edge variable width track – Einzackenschrift bei Lichtton
single-frame release – Einzelbildauslöser
single lens reflex camera – einäugige Spiegelreflexkamera
single perforated film – einseitig perforiertes Filmmaterial
single-picture action – Einergang
single, single shot – Aufnahme mit einem Darsteller
single system – Einbandsystem
single-wire cable – einadriges Kabel
size – Größe
skeleton diagram – Prinzipschema
skew – Bandzugregelung
slate – Filmklappe, Klappe, Synchronklappe
slave-recorder – Zuspielrekorder
slide – Diapositiv
slide carrier, slide mount – Diarahmen
slide projector – Diaprojektor
slide tray – Diamagazin

sliding base plate – Nivellierplatte
slippage of sound to picture – unbeabsichtigter Ton-Bild-Versatz
slit diaphragm – Schlitzblende
slit image – Spaltbild
slo-mo disk – Zeitlupenscheibe
slot – Sendezeit
slow motion (*slo mo*) – Zeitlupe
to slur – Silben verschlucken
smearing effect – Nachziehen, Nachzieheffekt
smoke gun – Nebelmaschine
smoke pot – Rauchpfanne
snackbar – Kantine
snap-shot – Schnappschuß
snoot – Tute für Scheinwerfer
snoot and white wash (*slang*) – ausgefressenes Negativ (*slang*)
socket – Steckdose
soft bromide paper – weiches Bromsilberpapier
soft focus – leichte Unschärfe als künstlerischer Effekt
soft focus lens – Weichzeichnerobjektiv
solar radiation – Sonnenstrahlung
soldering connexion – Lötverbindung
soldering iron – Lötkolben
soldering joint – Lötstelle
sold-out theatre – ausverkauftes Kino
solution – Lösung
solvent power – Auflösungsvermögen
sound – Ton
sound advance – beabsichtigter Ton-Bild-Versatz
sound apparatus room – Tonregieraum
sound carrier – Tonträger
sound change-over – Tonüberblendung
sound channel – Tonkanal
sound check – Tonprobe
sound department – Tonabteilung
sound editing – Tonschnitt
sound editor – Toncutter
sound effects – Geräusche
sound effect technican – Geräuschemacher

sound energy – Tonquelle
sound engineer – Toningenieur
sound equipment – Tonausrüstung
sound exiter lamp – Tonlampe
sound fade – Tonabblende
sound fader – Tonregler
sound fading – Tonüberblendung
sound film – Tonfilm
sound gobo – Schallblende
sound head – Tonabtasteinrichtung, Tonlaufwerk
sound intermediate frequency – Tonzwischenfrequenz
sound level – Tonpegel
sound level check – Tonprobe
sound library – Tonarchiv
sound loop – Tonschleife
sound man – Tonmann
sound mixer – Tontechniker, Tonmischpult
sound mixing – Tonüberblendung
sound monitoring apparatus – Abhörtisch
sound negative – Tonnegativ
sound only – nur Ton, off (*slang*), off-Ton
sound operator – Tontechniker
sound perspective – Raumton
sound picture projector – Zweibandprojektor
sound positive – Tonpositiv
sound printer – Tonkopiermaschine
sound projector – Tonfilmprojektor
sound proof – schalldicht
sound recorder (US) – 1. Tonassistent
sound recording – Tonaufnahme (Vorgang)
sound recording studio – Tonstudio
sound recording system – Tonaufzeichnungsverfahren
sound record speeding – Aufnahmegeschwindigkeit für Ton
sound report – Tonbericht
sound reports sheet – Tonbericht
sound reproduction – Tonwiedergabe
sound reverberation – Nachhall
sound signal – Tonsignal

sound-slide show – Ton-Bildschau
sound stage – Tonstudio
sound start mark – Tonstartmarkierung
sound system – Tonapparatur
sound tape – Geräuschband
sound tape – Tonband
sound technics – Tontechnik
sound test – Tonprobe
sound track – Tonspur
sound track advance – beabsichtigter Ton-Bild-Versatz
sound track negative – Lichttonnegativ, Tonnegativ
sound track placement – Tonspurlage
sound track striping – Filmbespurung
source – Quelle
spacing of perforation holes – Abstand der Perforationslöcher
spaghetti (*slang*) – Filmsalat (*slang*)
spaghetti western – Italo-Western
spark (*slang*) – Elektriker
spatial sound – Raumton
speaker – Sprecher
to speak for audition – vorsprechen
special effects – Spezial-Effekte, Tricks
special effects generator – Trickmischer
special trick – Trick
spectacle picture – Ausstattungsfilm, »Mantel-und-Degen-Film«
speech band – Sprachband
speech processor – Kompressor
speed – Belichtungszeit, Empfindlichkeit, Filmempfindlichkeit, Lichtstärke eines Objektivs
speed of taking – Aufnahmegeschwindigkeit für Bild
speed rating – Belichtungszeit
spherical aberration – sphärische Aberration
spider – Stativspinne
spider box – Mehrfachsteckdose, Verteilerdose, Vielfachstecker, Steckleiste, Stromverteiler
spiral dissolve – spiralförmige Blende
spirit level – Wasserwaage
splash – Spratzer, Spritzfleck

splice bump – Klebestellengeräusch
splicer – Filmhobel
splicing and blooping – Kleben und Tonanlegen
splicing girl – Kleberin
split-focus shot – Schärfenverlagerung
split-image range-finder – Schnittbildentfernungsmesser
split reel – auseinanderschraubare Filmspule
split sound system – Parallelton-Verfahren
split spool – auseinanderschraubare Filmspule
spoken title – Sprechtitel
sponsored broadcast – Sponsorsendung
spooky movie – Horrorfilm
spool – Filmspule bei Kleinbildfilm
sport commentator – Sportkommentator
sports and events, sports news programs – Sportsendung
sports view-finder – Sportsucher
spot – Sendezeit
spot photometer – Spotmeter, Pistole (*slang*)
spot-wobbled – zeilenfrei
to spread – Überziehen
spring pressure plate – federnde Andruckplatte
sprocket – Zahntrommel
sprocket drum – Filmtransportrolle
sprocketed film base – perforierter Film
sprocket hole – Perforationsloch
sprocket wheel – Filmtransportrolle
spun glass – Raster
sputter – Spratzer
squeete lens – anamorphotisches Objektiv
stabilizer – Stabilisierbad
staff – Aufnahmestab
stage curtain – Bühnenvorhang
stage direction – Regiestab
stage hand – Atelierarbeiter
stage left – linke Bühnenseite
stage manager – Inspezient
stage of amplification – Verstärkungsstufe
stage right – rechts Bühnenseite

stage weight – Bühnengewicht
staggered tuning – gestaffelte Abstimmung
stain – Fleck
stand – Stativ
standard frequency – Normalfrequenz
standard magazine – Einheitsmagazin
standards conversion equipment, standards converter – Normwandler
standard stock – 35mm Rohfilm
»Stand by!« – »Achtung! Bereithalten!«
stand by – Aufnahmebereitschaft
stand-in – Double
starter, starting solution – Starterlösung
starting switch – Anlaßschalter
startmarking – Startmarkierung
start of shooting – Drehbeginn
»Start rolling!« – »Achtung, Aufnahme!« Anweisung an den MAZ-Techniker
static shot – Aufnahme ohne Kamerabewegung
station identification signal – Pausenzeichen
steadyness of image – Bildstand
steel bayonet mount – Stahlbajonettfassung
steep graduation – steile Graduation, hart
step down ring – Adapterring, Reduzierring, Reduzieradapter
step-up ring – Anpaßring
stereo acoustics – plastische Raumtonwirkung, Stereoakustik
stereo-mixer – Stereomischpult
stereophonic – stereofonisch
stereophonic sound – Stereoton
stereophony – Stereofonie
stereoscopic film – Stereotonfilm, Stereofilm
stereoscopic picture – Raumbild
stereoscopic projection – Stereoprojektion
stereoscopic television – räumliches Fernsehen
stereoscopy – Stereoskopie
sticking, sticking picture – Nachbild der Fernsehkamera
still camera – Standbildkamera
still photograph – Standfoto
still projection – Standbildprojektion

stills library – Bildarchiv
stills photographer – Standbildfotograf
stock – Fundus
stock shot – Archivaufnahme
stock solution – Stammlösung, Vorratslösung
stop – Blende, Blendenzahl
stop bath – Stoppbad, Unterbrechungsbad
to stop down – abblenden
stop fixer – Stopfixierbad
stop frame – Standbildverlängerung
stop-frame rostrum – Tricktisch
stop motion – Einergang, Zeitraffer
stop motion motor – Einzelbildmotor
stop setting – Blendeneinstellung
storage – Aufbewahrung, Lagerung
storage box – Aufbewahrunskasten
storing pocket for negatives – Negativtaschen
story – Geschichte
story writer – Dramaturg
straight rail – gerade Schiene
stray angle – Streuwinkel
stray light – Streulicht
streak – Schliere
to strike a set – die Dekoration abbauen
striplight – Rampenlicht
structure-born vibration – Körperschall
studio – Atelier, Filmstudio
studio allocation-schedule, studio bookings – Studiodisposition
studio camera – Studiokamera
studio decoration (GB) – Studiodekor
studio director – Studioregisseur
studio engineering – Studiotechnik
studio exteriors – Aufbau einer Außenszene im Studio
studio lamp – Scheinwerfer
studio lighting – Studioscheinwerfer
studio lights – Aufnahmelampe
studio lot – Filmgelände
studio management – Atelierleitung
studio manager – Studiodirektor

studio rent – Studiomiete
studio setting – Studioaufbau
studio shot – Studioaufnahme
studio supervising window – Regiefenster
stylist – Kostümberater
stylus force – Auflagegewicht
sub-aqua equipment – Ausrüstung für Unterwasseraufnahmen
subcarrier – Hilfsträger, Nebenträger, Zwischenträger
subcarrier beat – Störung des Hilfsträgers
subcarrier frequency – Hilfsträgerfrequenz
subcarrier offset – Chrominanzträgerversetzung
to subdivide – aufteilen, zerteilen
subjective camera treatment – Substitution
submarine camera – Unterwasserkamera
sub-plot – Nebenhandlung
subscriber – Kabelfernsehteilnehmer
substandard film – Schmalfilm
substandard film camera – Schmalfilmkamera
substandard film distribution – Schmalfilmverleih
substandard film projector – Schmalfilmprojektor
substandard film size – Schmalfilmformat
substractive color system – substraktives Farbverfahren
subtitle – Untertitel
to subtitle – untertiteln
succeedet shot – gelungene Aufnahme
successive frame exposure – Einzelbildaufnahme
sun gun – 250W Handleuchte
sunset light – Abendlicht
sunshade – Sonnenblende
superaudible frequency – Tonfrequenz oberhalb von 20kHz
super iconoscope – Superikonoskop, Zwischenbildikonoskop
to superimpose – einkopieren, überblenden, überlagern
superimposed image – überlagertes Bild
superimposed print – Fußtitelkopie, Kopie mit Untertiteln
superimposed title – einkopierter Titel
superimposition – Doppelbelichtung
super, supernumerary – Komparse
super trooper – Verfolgungsscheinwerfer

supervising set builder – leitender Filmarchitekt
supervision – künstlerische Oberleitung
supplementary film – Vorfilm
supplementary lens – Vorsatzlinse
supply reel – Abwickelrolle
supply unit – Netzteil
supply voltage – Speisespannung
supporting part – Nebenrolle
supporting player – Nebendarsteller
surface mirror – halbdurchlässiger Spiegel
survey – Übersicht
to swallow – Silben verschlucken
sweep circuit – Zeitablenkschaltung
sweep device – Abtastvorrichtung
sweep frequency – Kippfrequenz, Wobbelfrequenz
sweep generator, sweep oszillator – Kippgenerator, Kipposzilloskop, Zeitablenkgenerator,
sweep voltage – Kippschaltung, Zeitablenkspannung
swinging burst – alternierender Burst
swish dissolve – Überblendung zweier Reißschwenks
swish pan – Reißschwenk
switch – Schalter
switch contact – Schaltkontakt
switcher – Bildtechniker, Bildmischer
switching schedule – Schaltplan
sync advance – beabsichtigter Ton-Bild-Versatz
sync generator – Taktgeber
synchronised print – Filmkopie mit Lichttonspur, Kopie mit Ton
synchronizer – Synchronumroller
to synchronize two separate stripes of film – Filmmaterial und Cordbänder synchron anlegen
synchronizing mark – Synchronzeichen
synchronizing mark, sync mark – Synchronmarke
synchronizing rushes – Tonanlegen
synchronizing time – Hochlaufzeit
synchronous drive – synchroner Antrieb
synchronous motor – Synchronmotor
synchronous winder – Synchronumroller
syncing – Synchronität

sync leader – Startband
sync point – Synchronpunkt
sync pop – Synchronmarke
sync signal generator – Taktgeber
sync sound – O-Ton
synopsis – Exposé

T

tacky – klebrig
tail – Filmende
tail leader – Endband
take – Aufnahme, Einstellung
take-off drum, take-off roller – Vorwickelrolle
to take photoflash picture – Blitzlichtaufnahmen machen
to take the air – senden, über den Sender gehen
take-up carter – Vorwickelrolle
take-up reel – Abwickelrolle
take-up side – Aufwickelseite
taking lens – Aufnahmeobjektiv
talent agency – Künstleragentur
talent scout – Talentsucher
talkback circuit – Gegensprechleitung
talking film – Tonfilm
tally light – Signalleuchte an der Fernsehkamera
tally-light, tally – Rotlicht
tank – Entwicklungstank
tank development – Tankentwicklung
tape – Band, Metermaß, Maßband, Tonband
tape break – Bandriß
tape curvature – Banddehnung
tape drive – Laufwerk
tape for editing – Schnittmaterial
tape guidance – Spurhaltung
tape guide – Bandführung
tape hiss – Bandrauschen
»Tape is on speed!« – »MAZ läuft!«, Antwort des MAZ-Technikers auf »MAZ ab!«
tape leader – Startband
tape length indicator – Bandlängenanzeiger
tape library – Nur Ton, Tonarchiv
tape loop – Bandschleife
tape machine – Tonbandgerät
tape man – EB-Techniker

tape monitor switch – Mithörschalter
tape noise – Bandrauschen
tape position indicator – Bandstellenanzeiger
tape record – Bandaufnahme
tape recorder – Bandgerät
tape run – Bandlauf
tape run indicator – Bandlaufanzeige
tape slippage – Bandschlupf
tape speed – Bandgeschwindigkeit
tape splicer with double side cutter – Klebepresse für Bild- und Tonschnitt
tape tension – Bandzug
tape type B (type C) – Videoband für den 1-Zoll B-Standard (1-Zoll C-Standard)
target car – gefilmtes Fahrzeug. Wird vom »insert car« gezogen.
target layer – Speicherplattenschicht
T core – Filmkern or Bobby mit 50mm Durchmesser
teaching film – Unterrichtsfilm
team – Ensemble, Filmteam, Team
technical adviser – technischer Berater
technical credits – Vorspann mit den Namen der Mitwirkenden
technical director – Bildtechniker
technical operator – Tonmann
tee – Stativspinne
telecast – Fernsehsendung
telecaster – Fernsehanstalt
telecine – Filmabtaster
telecine machine – Filmabtaster
telegenic – telegen
telephoto lens – Teleobjektiv
telephoto range zoom lens – langbrennweitiges Zoomobjektiv
teleplay – Fernsehspiel
tele prompter – Prompter, Textgeber, Textprojektor
telescopic finder – Fernrohrsucher
telescopic floor stand – ausziehbares Bodenstativ, ausziehbares Lampenstativ, Klappstativ
to televise a film – einen Film senden, ausstrahlen
television archives – Fernseharchiv
television cameratruck – Fernsehaufnahmewagen

television chart – Fernsehtestbild
television director – Intendant einer Fernsehanstalt
television drama – Fernsehspiel
television engineering – Fernsehtechnik
television principles – Grundlagen des Fernsehens
television receiver – Fernsehgerät
television reporting van – Fernsehaufnahmewagen
television set – Fernsehgerät
television shooting script – Fernsehdrehbuch
television sports news – Sportschau
television standards – Fernsehnormen
television system converter – Normwandler
television test cart – Fernsehtestbild
television tube – Bildröhre
television tube image – Fernsehbild
temperature – Temperatur
tempex – Carnet
tenner – 10kW Lampe
terminal resistance – Abschlußwiderstand
test department – Prüffeld
testimonial – spezielle Art von Werbefilm mit Laiendarstellern
testing voltage – Prüfspannung
test pattern – Testbild
test signal – Meßsignal
test stripe – Farbbestimmungsprobe, Farbteststreifen
test take – Probeaufnahme
test unit – Prüfeinrichtung
to texture – veredeln
thickness of tape – Bandstärke
third answer print – 3. Korrekturkopie
thirty – 30-Sekunden Fernsehspot
35mm lens – Objektiv für 35mm Film
to thread – Film in die Kamera einlegen
3-D film – 3-D Film, dreidimensionaler Film
3-gun picture tube – 3-strahl Fernsehröhre
3-legged stand – Dreibeinstativ
3-phase current – Drehstrom
three-shot – Aufnahme mit drei Darstellern

three-strip – Technicolorverfahren
3-tube camera – Dreiröhrenkamera
threshold of pain – Schmerzgrenze
to throw focus – die Schärfe nachziehen
ticket – Eintrittskarte
tight shot – Großaufnahme
tight shot – Nahaufnahme
to tilt – neigen, vertikal schwenken
tiltable view-finder – schwenkbarer Sucher
tilt head – Neigekopf, Kameraneiger
tilting – Kameraneigung
tilting head, tilting platform, tilt top, tiltop – Neigekopf, Kinoneiger
timbre – Klangfarbe
time accelerator – Zeitraffer
time base – Zeitbasis, Zeitablenkung, Kippablenkung, X-Achse
time base corrector – Zeitfehlerkorrektur
time base deflection – Zeitablenkung
time base generator – zeitabhängiger Kippgenerator, Kippgenerator, Kipposzilloskop, Zeitablenkgenerator
time base voltage – Kippschaltung, Zeitablenkspannung
time-code reader – Timecodeleser
timed print (US) – lichtbestimmte Kopie, Korrekturkopie
time lapse – Zeitraffer
time lapse recorder – Zeitrafferrekorder
time lapse shooting – Zeitrafferaufnahme, unterdrehen
time of transmission – Sendezeit
timer – Lichtbestimmer im Kopierwerk, Schaltuhr
timing light – Kopierlicht
timing, timing of print light, timing of printing light – Lichtbestimmung
tinged – farbstichig
to tint – einfärben
tissue – Abdeckfolie, Abschminktuch
title – Titel, Vorspann, Nachspann
title background – Titeluntergrund
title card, title cartoon – Titelvorlage
title drum – Rolltitelgerät
title-link – Zwischentitel
title negative – Titelnegativ

title photographing – Titelaufnahme

tits and asses (*slang*) – Fernsehprogramm mit jungen Mädchen

tonal proportions – Grauverhältnis

tone color – Klangfarbe

tone control – Tonhöhenregler

tone pitch – Tonhöhe

too contrasty – knochig (*slang*), zu hart, zu kontrastreich

toon (*slang*) – Trickfilmfigur

topical film – Reportage

top loop – obere Filmschleife

top-player – Hauptdarsteller

total view – Gesamtansicht, Übersichtsaufnahme, Totale

touring cinema – Wanderkino

tourist film – Reisefilm

T-powered microphone – tonadergespeistes Mikrofon

trace interval – Zeilenabtastdauer

tracker – Dollyfahrer

tracking – Auflagemaß, Spurhaltung

tracking force – Auflagegewicht

tracking shot – Fahraufnahme mit Dolly, Kamerafahrt

track placement, track position – Spurlage

trade press – Fachpresse

trade show – Interessentenvorführung

trailer – Trailer, Vorspannfilm

trainee – Praktikant, Volontär

to transcribe, to transfer – überspielen

transfer – Überspielung

transfocator – Gummilinse (*slang*), Transfokator, Varioobjektiv, Zoomobjektiv

transitional scene – Überleitungsszene

transmission – Fernsehübertragung

transmission chain – Senderkette

transmission standard – Sendenorm, Übertragungsnorm

transmission time – Sendezeit

transmission tower – Sendeturm

transmitter – Sender

transmitter amplifier – Mikrofonvorverstärker

transmitting power – Sendeleistung

transparency – Diapositiv, Transparenz
transparent color – Lasurfarbe
transparent mirror – halbdurchlässiger Spiegel
transparent screen for rear projection – Rückprojektionswand
transparent to ultraviolet – ultraviolet durchlässig
transportation – Produktionsfahrer
transport case – Tragetasche
transversal recording – Querspurverfahren
transversal scratch – Querschramme
travel expenses – Reisekosten
traveling mask, traveling matte – Wandermaske
traveling shot – Fahraufnahme
travelling – Kamerafahrt
travelling key – nachgeführtes Führungslicht
travelling man – Dollyfahrer
travel shot – Fahraufnahme vom Dolly
treatment – Abhandlung, Treatment
treatment of the script – Drehbuchentwurf
treble – Höhen
treble boost – Höhenanhebung
treble cut – Höhenabsenkung
triangle – Stativspinne, Beleuchtung mit 3 Lampen
trick button – Tricktaste
trick shot – Trickaufnahme
trick table – Tricktisch
trick work – Trickarbeit
tricolor tube – 3-Strahlröhre
trigger – Auslöser
trims – Schnittmaterial
triple-track recorder – Aufnahmegerät für drei Spuren
tripod – Stativ
tripod case – Stativfuteral
tripod head – Stativkopf
tripod leg – Stativbein
tripod lengthening – Stativverlängerung
tripod quick-coupling – Stativschnellkupplung
tripod turn – Stativgewinde

trolly – Kamerawagen
truck – Dolly
trucking title – Fahrtitel
truck wheel – Schienenrad
truncated picture – abgekaschtes Bild
T-shoe – Klemmschuh, Zubehörschuh
T-stop – T-Blendenwert
tube – Bildröhre, Röhre
tube characteristic – Röhrenkennlinie
tubed – röhrenbestückt
tube hiss, tube noise – Röhrenrauschen
tubular light – Soffite
tulle – Tüll
tuner – Empfänger, Kanalwähler
tungsten light – Glühlicht, Kunstlicht
tuning – Abstimmung
tuning variometer – Abstimmgerät
»Turn over!« – »Kamera ab!« Anweisung an den Kameramann
turnstile aerial – Kreuzdipol
turntable – Drehteller, Plattenspieler
to turn yellow – vergilben
turret head – Objektivrevolver
TV broadcaster – Fernsehanstalt
TV frequency transposer (converter) – Fernsehkanalumsetzer
TV shooting script – Fernsehdrehbuch
tweeter (US) – Hochtonlautsprecher
20/20, best view – bester Visus, optimales Sehvermögen
twilight shot – Aufnahme im Halbdunkel
twin lens – Zwillingsobjektiv
twin-lens reflex camera – zweiäugige Spiegelreflexkamera
two-bath developer – Zweibadentwickler
two blade shutter – Zwischenflügel einer Umlaufblende
two-field picture – Bild, das aus zwei Teilbildern im Zeilensprungverfahren gebildet wird, beide Halbbilder eines Fernsehbildes, Vollbild
two-shot – Aufnahme mit zwei Darstellern, amerikanische Einstellung, Halbnaheinstellung, Zweiereinstellung
two track projector – Zweibandprojektor
Tyler mount – Hubschrauberaufhängung
typecast – Doppelgänger

U

ultra-short wave reciever – UKW Empfänger
ultra soft – ultraweich
ultraviolet – ultraviolett
unabridged – ungekürzt
unbalanced microphone input – unsymetrischer Mikrofoneingang
uncut tape – Schnittmaterial, ungeschnittenes Videoband
under – Hintergrundmusik
to undercrank – unterdrehen
underdevelop – Unterentwicklung
under-exposure – Unterbelichtung
underfootage – Unterlänge
undermodulation – zu geringe Aussteuerung
understudy – Double eines Darstellers
undervoltage – Unterspannung
underwater blimp, underwater housing – Unterwassergehäuse
underwater camera – Unterwasserkamera
unestablished staff contract – Zeitvertrag
unexposed film – Rohfilmmaterial, unbelichtetes Filmmaterial
unidirectional microphone – Richtmikrofon, Kanone (*slang*)
union – Gewerkschaft
unit – Filmteam
unit manager – Aufnahmeleiter
unit manager, unit production manager – Aufnahmeleiter
universal enlarger – Universalvergrößerer
universal focus lens – Fixfokusobjektiv
universal follow focus mechanism – Universal-Schärfenzieheinrichtung
universal lens support – universal Objektivstütze
to unload – Film auslegen
unmodulated density – Ruheschwärzung
unmodulated track – Ruhespur
unsharp image – unscharfes Bild
to unsqueeze – entzerren
unsteady contact – Wackelkontakt
unweighted signal-to-noise ratio – Fremdspannungsabstand
upper film loop – obere Filmschleife

upright image – aufrechtstehendes Bild
useful power – Nutzleistung
utmost sharpness – höchste Schärfe

V

van – MAZ-Wagen

variable area sound recording system – Transversalverfahren

variable area track – Zackenschrift

variable condenser – Drehkondensator

variable density recording – Sprossenschrift bei Lichtton

variable focus lens – Gummilinse (*slang*), Transfokator, Varioobjektiv, Zoomobjektiv

variable shutter – verstellbare Sektorenblende

variable-speed motor – Handregelmotor, Motor mit regelbarer Geschwindigkeit, regelbarer Motor

variation – Abweichung

variofocal lens – Gummilinse (*slang*), Transfokator, Varioobjektiv, Zoomobjektiv

vault – Filmbunker

vault storage for film – Filmbunker

vectorscope – Vektorskop

veiling – Schleier

velocity – Geschwindigkeit

velveting sound – Reinigung der Tonbänder mit zwei Samttüchern

vertex picture – Hochformat

vertical hold control – Bildfangregler

vertical hunting (GB) – Bildpumpen

vertical-line – Lotrechte

vertical shift – Hoch/Tiefverschiebung

video – Video

video/film synchronizer – Phasenschieber

video alignment – Videoabgleich

videoannouncer – Ansager, Fernsehansager

video bus – Fernsehaufnahmewagen, MAZ-Wagen

video cable – Videokabel

video carrier – Videoträgerwelle

video cartridge recorder, video cassette recorder – Videokassettenrekorder

video channel – Bildkanal

video control room – Bildregieraum

video detector – Videobildgleichrichter

video disc – Bildplatte
video distributor – Videoverteiler
videoengineer – Bildingenieur
video final stage – Videoendstufe
video frequency – Videofrequenz
video head – Videokopf
video head wheel – Videokopfrad
video intensity – Bildhelligkeit
video interconnection point – Übergabepunkt an Fernsehleitungen
video locking – Videoverkopplung
video looping – durchschleifen des Videosignals
video matrix – Videoverteiler
video mixing desk – Bildmischpult
video operator – Fernsehtechniker
video output – Videoausgangssignal
video quality control – Videomeßdienst
video reception – Videoempfang
videorecording – Videoaufzeichnung
video signal – BAS-Signal, Videosignal
video sub carrier – Farbhilfsträger
video switch – Hartschnittumschalter, Bildumschalter
video-tape dubbing – Überspielung, kopieren
video tape library – Videothek
video tape operator – Videotechniker
video tape recorder – Videorekorder
video tape type B (type C) – Videoband für den 1-Zoll B-Standard (1-Zoll C-Standard)
videotaping – mit Video aufnehmen
video technican – Fernsehtechniker
video test signal generator – Videoprüfsignalgeber
video track – Bildspur, Videospur
video transmitter – Fernsehsender
video viewer – Fernsehzuschauer
vidicon – Vidikon
view camera – Großformatkamera, Studiokamera
viewer – Laufbildbetrachter, Zuschauer
view-finder – Sucher
view-finder eyepiece – Sucherokular
view-finder frame – Sucherkasch

view-finder lens – Sucherobjektiv

view-finder magnifier – Sucherlupe

view-finder mismatch – Abweichung zwischen dem Sucherbild und dem Bildfenster

viewing angle – Betrachtungswinkel

viewing figure – Sehbeteiligung

viewing filter – Kontrastglas

viewing lens – Sucherobjektiv

viewing screen – Bildschirm

viewing theatre – Vorführraum

vignette – Kasch, Maske, Vignette

vintage movie – Kintopp (*slang*)

violet – violett

virgin, virgin tape – frisches Bandmaterial, Leerband

virtual image – virtuelles Bild

vision – Sehvermögen, Vision

vision break – Bildausfall

vision carrier – Bildträger

vision control room – Bildregieraum

vision control supervisor – Bildingenieur

vision mixer – Bildtechniker

vision mixer panel – Videoschaltpult

vision to sound-carrier spacing – Bild-Tonträgerabstand

vista shot – Fernaufnahme, Gesamtaufnahme, Totale

visual acuteness (US) – Sehschärfe

visualization – Sichtbarmachung, Umsetzung

voice over – Sprecher über einer fremdlänmdischen Fassung, die im Hintergrund hörbar bleibt

voltage – Spannung, Stromspannung

voltage adapter – Spannungswähler

voltage amplification – Spannungsverstärkung

voltage stabilization – Spannungsstabilisierung

volume – Lautstärke, Tonpegel

volume control – Lautstärkeregeler

volume indicator – Aussteuerungsanzeige

VTR in camera – Rekorderkamera

W

waist level finder – Faltlichtschachtsucher
walkie-talkie – Sprechfunkgerät
walk on 1 – Komparse
walk on 2 – Kleindarsteller
walk-on fee – Komparsengage
walk-through – Probedurchlauf
walla-walla – allgemeines Gemurmel in einer Massenszene
wardrobe supervisor (GB) – Kostümberater
war film – Kriegsfilm
warm colors – warme Farben
warming-up time, warm-up time – Aufheizzeit
wash – wässern, Wässerungsbad
waste – Verschnitt
watered silk – Moiré-Effekt
water stain – Wasserfleck
wave crest – Wellenberg
wave form monitor – Bildkontrollgerät, Kontrolloszilloskop
wavelength – Wellenlänge
weather protector cover – Wetterschutzhaube
wedge range-finder – Keilentfernungsmesser
western – Western
wet – naß
wet gate – Naßkopierfenster
wheeled skid – Fahrspinne (Stativ)
wheeled tee, wheeled tie-down, wheeled triangle – Fahrspinne
whip pan – Reißschwenk
white balance – Weißabgleich
white balance indicator – Weißabgleichanzeige
white clipping – Weißwertbegrenzung
white film, white leader – Weißfilm
white level – Weißwert
white noise – Röhrenrauschen, weißes Rauschen
white spacing – Weißfilm
white-to-black frequency deviation – Frequenzbandbreite
wide-angle bellows – Weitwinkelbalgen

wide-angle effect – Weitwinkeleffekt
wide-angle lens – Weitwinkelobjektiv
wide-angle matte box – Weitwinkelkompendium
wide-angle zoom lens – Weitwinkelzoomobjektiv
wide-range amplifier – Breitbandverstärker
wide-screen – Breitwand
wide-screen aperture film gate – Breitwandformatbildfenster
wide-screen film – Breitwandfilm
wide-screen system – Breitwandverfahren
width of cut – Schnittweite
width of film – Filmbreite
width of the frequency band – Frequenzbandbreite
wig-maker – Perückenmacher
wigwag – Rotlichtwarnlampe vor Studios
wild camera – ungeblimpte Filmkamera
wild motor – Motor mit variabler Geschwindigkeit, Handregelmotor
wild picture – Aufnahme ohne Synchronton, stumme Einstellung
wild recording – asynchrone Tonaufnahme
wild sound – Atmo
wildtrack – Tonaufnahme ohne Bild
wild-wall (*slang*) – Sprungwand
wild west film – Western
to wind – wickeln
wind gag – Mikrofonwindschutz
winding – Wicklung
winding bench – Umrolltisch
wind machine – Windmaschine
window program – Fensterprogramm
window unit – kleiner Ü-Wagen, Reportagefahrzeug
wind protection – Windschutz
wind shielding properties – Windgeräuschunterdrückung
windsock – Windmuff
wind-up crank – Filmtransportkurbel
wing – Kulisse
to wipe – blenden, löschen von Magnetbändern
wipe – Trickblende, Wischblende
to wipe-off – abblenden
to wipe-on – aufblenden

wireless microphone – drahtloses Mikrofon, Funkmikrofon
wiremann – Elektriker
wire net scrim – Drahtgaze
wire release – Drahtauslöser
without contrast – flau
wooden tripod – Holzstativ
woofer – Baßlautsprecher, Tieftonlautsprecher
working blade – Abdeckflügel einer Umlaufblende
working conditions – Arbeitsbedingungen
working instructions – Arbeitsrichtlinien, Bedienungsvorschrift
working solution – Arbeitslösung
working title – Arbeitstitel, vorläufiger Titel
working volt, working voltage – Arbeitsspannung, Betriebsspannung
working wing of a rotating shutter – Arbeitsflügel einer Umlaufblende
work light – Arbeitslicht, Bühnenlicht
work print, working print – Arbeitskopie, AK, Klatsche (*slang*), Muster, Schnittkopie
world premier – Welturaufführung
worm drive, worm gear – Schneckengetriebe
worm's eye view – Froschperspektive
wow – Jaulen
wow and flutter – Tonhöhenschwankungen durch unregelmäßigen Bandlauf
wows of sound – Jaulen des Tons
wrap – Ende eines Drehtags
»Wrap!«; »It's a wrap!« – »Gestorben!« (*slang*), akzeptierte Aufnahme
wrinkling of gelatin – Runzelkorn
wrist strap – Handschlaufe
writer – Autor, Verfasser
writer's own film – Autorenfilm
writing speed – Aufzeichnungsgeschwindigkeit

X

X-Certificate (GB) – Film, der für Jugendliche ab 16 Jahren freigegeben ist
X-contact – X-Kontakt
X-deflection – Zeitablenkung
X-rated film – indizierter Film, nicht jugendfreier Film
X-ray cinematography – Röntgenkinematografie
X-ray photography – Röntgenfotografie

Y

yellow – Gelb
yellow discoloration, yellowing – Vergilbung
yellow tinged – gelbstichig
Y-level – Schwarzwert
young artists – Nachwuchs
Y-signal – Farbluminanzsignal (4,5 MHz)

Z

Z core – Filmkern oder Bobby mit 75mm Durchmesser
zeppelin, zeppelin windscreen – Zeppelin (*slang*), Korbwindschutz
zero adjustment – Nulleinstellung
zero position – Nullage
zip pan – Reißschwenk
zone focusing – Schnappschußeinstellung
zone of sharpness – Tiefenschärfebereich
to zoom – zoomen, die Brennweite verändern
zoom-away shot – aufziehen, aufziehende Aufnahme, die Brennweite verkürzen
zoom blimp – Objektivblimb, Objektivschallschutz
zoom handle – Zoomhebel
zooming in the course of exposure – während der Belichtung zoomen
zoom-in shot – verdichten, verdichtende Aufnahme, die Brennweite verlängern
zoom lens – Gummilinse (*slang*), Transfokator, Variooobjektiv, Zoomobjektiv
zoom lever – Zoomhebel
zoom-out shot – aufziehen, aufziehende Aufnahme, die Brennweite verkürzen
zoom range, zoom ratio – Brennweitenbereich
zoom rod – Zoomhebel

Abkürzungen

A

A	Ampère
AAAA	American Association of Advertising Agencies
AAAA	Associated Actors and Artists of America
A.A.C.	Austrian Association of Cinematographers
ABC	American Broadcasting Company
ABC	Asahi Broadcasting Company
ABC	Australian Broadcasting Company
ABC	automatic beam control
ABO	automatic beam optimiser
ABS	Association of Broadcasting and Allied Staff, GB
ABTT	Association of British Theatre Technicians
ABU	Asia-Pacific Broadcast Union
AC	alternative current
ACAR	Arab Center for Audience Research
ACC	automatic color control
A.C.E.	American Society of Cinema Editors
ACE	advanced conversion equipment
ACR	acceptable contrast ratio
ACSA	Allied Communication Security Agency
ACT	action for children
ACT	automatic code time
ACTT	Association of Cinematograph, Television and allied Technicians
ACTV	advanced compatible TV system
ACVL	Association of Cinema and Video Laboratories, USA
AD	assistant director
AD	analog-to-digital
ADAC	advanced digital adaptive converter
ADC	analog-to-digital converter
A2	Antenne 2, Frankreich
ADMAC	Austrian Documentation Centre for Media and Communication Research
ADN	Allgemeiner Deutscher Nachrichtendienst
ADO	Ampex digital optics
ADR	automatic dialogue replacement
ADT	automatic double tracking
A/DU	Analog-digital Umsetzer

AEFA	Association Euopéenne du Film d'Animation (Belgien
AES	Audio Engineering Society, USA
AEV	Aufnahmeentzerrverstärker
AF	audio frequency
AFA	automatische Feinabstimmung
AFC	automatic frequency control
AFF	Aktion Funk und Fernsehen
AFI	American Film Institute
AfK	Arbeitsgemeinschaft für Kommunikationsforschung
AFM	American Federation of Musicians
AFM	assistant floor manager
AFMA	American Film Marketing Association, USA
AFN	American Forces Network
AFP	Agence France Press
AfP	Archiv für Presserecht
AFPF	Association Française de Production de Films
AFT	automatic fine tuning
AFTR	American Forces Television and Radio
AFTRA	American Federation of Television and Radio Artists
AGB	Audits of Great Britain, for audience research in TV, video and cable, GB
AGC	automatic gain control
AG.MA	Arbeitsgemeinschaft Media-Analyse
AG N D	Arbeitsgemeinschaft Neuer Deutscher Spielfilmproduzenten
AGS	automatische Grauwertstabilisierung
ags	Wissenschaftliche Arbeitsgemeinschaft für Studio- und Senderfragen
AGVA	American Guild of Variety Artists
AI	Aussteuerinstrument
AIBD	Asia Pacific Institute for Broadcasting Development
AICP	Association of Independent Commercial Producers, USA
A.I.D.	Alliance Internationale de la Distribution par Cable
AIEE	American Institute of Electrical Engineers
AIERI	Association Internationale des Etudes et Recherches sur l'Information
AIR	Asociaçión Interamericana de Radiodufisión
AIRC	Association of Independent Radio Contractors, GB
AK	Arbeitskopie
AKK	Anstalt für Kabelkommunikation

AKUT	Arbeitskreis Unterrichtstechnik im ZVEI
AKW	Arbeitskreis Werbefernsehen der deutschen Wirtschaft
ALC	automatic level control
A/lm	Ampère/Lumen
ALR	Arbeitskreis Fotolabortechnik und Reproduktion
A/m	Ampère/Meter
AM	Amplitudenmodulation
AMI	Association for Multi-Image International
AMIC	Asian Mass Communication Research and Information Centre
AMIP	American Market for International Programs
AMPAS	Academy of Motion Picture Arts and Sciences
AMPTP	Association of Motion Pictures and Television Producers
AMS	advanced memory system
ANA	Association of National Advertisers
ANB	Asahi National Broadcasting Company
ANL	automatic noise-limiting
ANN	Asian News Network
ANP	Algemeen Nederlandsch Perbureau
ANPA	American Newspaper and Publishers Association
ANRS	automatic noise reduction system
ANSA	Agenzia Nazionale Stampa
ANSI	American National Standards Institute
Antiope	Acquisition Numérique et Télévisualisation d'Images Organisées en Pages d'Ecriture
AOR	Atlantic Ocean Region
AP	Associated Press
APA	Austria Presse Agentur
APC	automatic phase control
APD	avalanche photo-diode
APO	action print only
APP	Arbeitskreis Portrait – Photografie
APRS	Association of Professional Recording Studios
APS	automatic program search
APT	automatic picture transmission
AQL	acceptable quality level
ARB	American Research Bureau
ARD	Arbeitsgemeinschaft der öffentlich-rechtlichen Rundfunkanstalten der Bundesrepublik Deutschland
ARQ	automatic-repeat-request

ARRI	Arnold & Richter
ARS	Akademie für musische Erziehung und Medienerziehung
ARW	Arbeitsgemeinschaft Rundfunkwerbung der Werbefernseh- und Werbefunkgesellschaften der ARD
ASA	American National Standards Institute
asb	Apostilb
ASBU	Arab States Broadcasting Union
A.S.C.	American Society of Cinematographers
ASCAP	American Society of Composers, Authors and Publishers
ASIN	Acción de Sistemas Informativos Nacionales
ASMOS	automatisierte Senderegie Mono oder Stereo
asp	Apostilb
ASR	automatische Senderegie
ATE	automatic test equipment
ATF	automatic track following
ATS	automatic transmission system
ATSC	Advanced Television Systems Committee, USA
ATTS	automatic-tape-time-select-system
AÜ	Außenübertragung
AUDS	Arbeitsgemeinschaft der Unterhaltungsabteilungen deutschsprachiger Sender
AV	audio-visuell, audio-visual
AVA	Audio Visual Association, GB
AVAMA	Audio Visual & Allied Manufacturers Association, GB
AVC	automatic volume control
AVD	Association of Video Dealers, GB
AVR	automatische Verstärkungsregelung
AVRO	Allgemeene Vereeniging Radio Omroep
AWI	Arbeitsgemeinschaft Werbe-, Mode-, Industriefotografie
AWR	Adventist World Radio

B

BABE	Broadcasting Across the Barriers of European Languages, CH
BABT	British Approvals Board for Telecommunications
BAFTA	British Academy of Film and Television Arts
BAPSA	Broadcast Advertising Producers Society of America
BAR	Broadcast Advertisers Report

BARB	Broadcasters Audience Research Board, GB
BAS-Signal	Bild-Austast-Synchron-Signal
BBC	British Broadcast Corporation
BBFC	British Board of Film Classification
BBK	Breitband-Kommunikation
BCAVM	British Catalogue of AV Material
BCI	broadcast interference
BCNZ	Broadcasting Corporation of New Zealand
BCU	big close-up shot
bd	Baud
BDF	Bundesverband Deutscher Fernsehproduzenten, D
BDW	Deutscher Kommunikationsverband
BDZV	Bundesverband Deutscher Zeitungsverleger
BEAB	British Electrotechnical Approval Board
BELGA	Belgisch Pers-Telegraaf-Agentschap
BERKOM	Berliner Kommunikationsnetz zur Erprobung der Breitbandkommunikation
BETA	Broadcasting and Entertainment Trades Alliance
BFBS	British Forces Broadcasting Service
BFI	British Film Institut
BFN	British Forces Network
B.F.S.	Bundesverband Filmschnitt – Cutter
BFTPA	British Film & Television Producers Association
Bg	background
BIEM	Bureau International de L'Edition Mécanique
BILD	Bureau international de liaison et de documentation
BIPM	Bureau international des poids et mesures
BITEG	Bildschirmtext-Erprobungs-Gesetz
BK	Breitband-Kommunikation
BKS	Bundesverband Kabel und Satellit
BKSTS	British Kinematograph Sound & Television Society
BLM	Bayerisch Landeszentrale für Medien
BNC	blimped noiseless camera
BO	box office
B.P.	backprojection
BP	battery pack
BPA	Bundespresseamt
BPEG	The Association of British Manufacturers of Photographic, Cine & Audio-Visual Equipment

BPI	Bundesverband der phonographischen Industrie
BPI	British Phonographic Industry
BPRT	Bundesverband privater Rundfunk- und Telekommunikation
BPS	Bundesprüfstelle für jugendgefährdende Schriften
BR	Bayerischer Rundfunk
BREEMA	British Radio and Electronic Equipment Manufacturers Association
BRT	Belgische Radio en Televisie, Belgien
BRW	Bayrische Rundfunkwerbung
BSC	British Society of Cinemathographers, GB
BSI	British Standards Institution
BSS	British Standards Specificationt
BT	Bulgarsko Radio i Televidenie, Bulgarien
BT	British Telecom
BTL	behind the lens
BTS	Broadcast Television Systems
BTV	Bangladesh Television
Btx	Bildschirmtext
BUFI	Bundesvereinigung des Deutschen Films
BUFVC	British Universities Film and Video Council
BVA	British Videogram Association
BVC	Bundesverband Filmschnitt
BVK	Bundesverband Kamera
BVU	broadcast video u-matic
B/W	black and white
BWF	Berliner Werbefunk

C

Ca	Computeranimation
CaBC	Caribbean Broadcasting Corporation
CABSC	Canadien Advanced Broadcast Systems Commitee
CAE	Radio Canadian Europe
CANA	Caribbean News Agency
CAR	Cadena Azul de Radiodifusión, Spanien
CAR	central apparatus room
CATA	Community Antenna Television Association
CATV	Community Antenna Television System

CATV	cable television
CAV	constant angular velocity
cAVcom	Centrum-AV-Communication
CBA	Commonwealth Broadcasting Association
CBC	Canadian Broadcasting Corporation
CBN	Christian Broadcast Network
CBS	Columbia Broadcasting Systems
CBU	Caribbean Broadcasting Union
CC	compact-cassette
CCD	charge-coupled devices
CCDS	Centre Commun d'Etudes de Télévision et de Télécommunication
CC-Filter	color compensating filter
CCIR	Comité Consulatif International des Radio-Communication
CCIS	Coaxial Cable Information System
CCITT	Consultative Committee for International Telegraphy & Telephones
CCR	central control room
CCTV	closed-circuit television
CCU	camera control unit
CD	compact disk
CD-I	compact disk interactive
CdS	Cadmiumsulfid
CD-V	compact disk – video
CEA	Cinema Exhibitors Association, GB
CECOM	Central European Mass Communication Research and Documentation Centre
CED	capacitance electronic disk
CEN	Central Educational Network
CENELEC	European Committee for Electrotechnical Standardisation
CEPT	Conférence Européene des Administrations des Postes et des Télécommunications
CET	Council for Educational Technology, GB
CETS	Conférence Européenne des Télécommunications par Satellite
CFM	control function memory
CH	channel
CHN	Cable Health Network
CHUT	cable household using TV
cid	compact iodide daylight

C.I.E.	Commission Internationale de l'Eclairage
CIE	International Commision on Illumination
CIESPAL	Centro International de Estudos Superiores de Communicatión para Américana Latina
CILECT	Centre International de Liason des Ecoles de Cinéma et de Télévision
CIRM	Comité International Radio Maritime
CIT	Central Independent Television
CIT	Convention Internationale des Télécommunications
CLR	Compagnie Luxembourgeoise de Radiodiffusion
CLT	Compagnie Luxembourgeoise de Télédiffusion
CLV	constant linear velocity
CMRR	common mode rejection ratio
CMRT	Corporación Mexicana de Radio y Televisión
CNC	Centre National de Cinématographie, F
CNCL	Commission Nationale de la Cinématographie, Frankreich
CNN	Cable News Network
CNR	carrier-to-noise ratio
COMMAG	combined magnetic sound
COMOPT	combined optical sound
COMSAT	Communications Satellite Corporation
CONTAM	Committee on Nationwide Television Audience Measurement
CP	construction permit
CP	Cinema Products
cpa	Christliche Presse-Akademie
CPB	Corporation for Public Broadcasting
CPF	Canal Plus France
CP-Filter	color printing filter
cps	cycles per second
CPU	Commenwealth Press Union
CRI	color-reversal intermediate
CRT	cathode ray tube
CS	close shot
CSI	compact source iodide
CSO	color separation overlay
CST	Commission Supérieure Technique du Cinéma Française
CTA	Cable Television Association, GB
CTB	color temperature blue
CTCM	chrominance time-compression multiplexing

CTDM	compressed time division multiplex
CTI	colore transient improvment
CTL	control track longitudinal
CTN	Club Theatre Network, USA
CTO	color temperature orange
ctrl	control
CTS	Communications Technology Satellite
CTV	Canadian Television
CTW	Children's Television Workshop
CU	close up
CV	Central-Verband Deutscher Photographen
CVC	compact video cassette
CvD	Chef vom Dienst
CyBC	Cyprus Broadcasting Corporation, Zypern

D

D2-Mac	Duobinär-Multiplex Analog Component
DA	directional antenna
DAC	digital-analog-converter
DAT	digital audio tape
DAT	Diaabtaster
dB	Dezibel
DBS	direct broadcasting satellite
DC	direct current
DCR	digital cassette recorder
DCT	Diskreter Cosinus Transfer
ddp	Deutscher Depeschendienst
DEFA	Deutsche Film AG, jetzt: Deutsche Filmgesellschaft
DFF	Deutscher Fernsehfunk
DFFB	Deutsche Film- und Fernsehakademie Berlin
DFS	Deutscher Fernmeldesatellit
DFZ	Deutsches Filmzentrum
DGA	Directors Guild of America
DGPh	Deutsche Gesellschaft für Photographie
DIANE	Direct Information Access Network Europe
DIF	Deutsches Institut für Filmkunde

DIN	Deutsches Institut für Normung
DIT	Digital Image Technician
DJU	Deutsche Journalisten Union
DJV	Deutscher Journalisten Verband
DLF	Deutschlandfunk
DLM	Direktorenkonferenz der Landesmedienanstalten
DMA	designed market area
DMR	Deutscher Musikrat
DMV	Deutscher Musikverleger-Verband
DPM	Dynamic Pixel Management
dpa	Deutsche Presseagentur
DR	Danmarks Radio
DRA	Deutsches Rundfunkarchiv
DRS	Fernsehen der deutschen und der rätoromanischen Schweiz
DTF	dynamic track following
DV	Digital Video
DVE	digitales Effektgerät
DVM	Digitalvoltmeter
DW	Deutsche Welle
DWRC	Deutscher Weltradio-Club

E

EA	Einzelantenne
EAP	elektronische Außenproduktion
EAVA	European Audio-visual Association
EB	electronic broadcasting, elektronische Berichterstattung
EB	end board
EBC	European Business Channel
EBC	Educational Broadcasting Corporation
EBR	electronic beam recording
EBS	Emergency Broadcast System
EBU	European Broadcasting Union
ECFA	Europäischer Kinderfilmverband
ECL	emitter coupled logic
ECN	Eastman color negative
ECPC	Electronic Cable Promission Commission
ECS	European Communications Satellite

ECU	extreme close up
EDTV	extended definition television
EDV	elektronische Datenverarbeitung
EE	electronic-to-electronic
EECO	videotape recorder editing equipment
EETPU	Electrical, Electronic, Telecommunications and Plumbing Union, GB
efdo	European Film Distribution Office
EFP	electronic field production
EFuSt	Erdfunkstelle
EHF	extremely high frequency
eht	extremely high tension
E.I.	exposure index
EIA	Electronic Industries Association, USA
EIAJ	Electronic Industries Association of Japan
EIRT	Ethnikon Idryma Radiophonias-Tileoraseos
EJ	electronic journalism
EKDM	Expertenkommission »Förderung neuer Kommunikationstechniken«
EKK	Europäischer Kulturkanal
EKM	Expertenkommission Neue Medien
EL	Elektrolumineszenz
ELCB	earth leakage circuit breakers
ELF	extremely low frequency
ELR	electronic line replacement
ELS	extreme long shot
EM	electronic mail
EMF	electromotive force
EMG	Euro Media Guaranties
ENG	electronic news gathering
ENR	Emisora Nacional de Radiodifusao, Portugal
ePAL	enhanced PAL
epd	Evangelischer Pressedienst
EPF	Erste Private Fernsehanstalt
EPG	Europäische Produktionsgemeinschaft
EPP	electronic post-production
EPR	electronic pin registration
ER	editor's report
ERP	effective radiated power

ERT	Elliniki Radiophonia Tikleorasi, Griechenland
ERTU	Egyptian Radio and Television Union
ESA	European Space Agency
ESG	electronic sports gathering
ESPN	Entertainment and Sports Programming Network
ESPRIT	European Strategic Research Program in Information Technology
ESRO	European Space Research Organisation
ETA	Educational Television Association, USA
ETB	elektrisches Farbtestbild
E-to-E	electronic-to-electronic
ETS	Einheitstonsystem
ETSA	European Television Services Association
ETV	educational television
EURIMAGE	Filminitiative of Council of Europe, F
EURIPA	European Information Providers Association
Eutelsat	European Telecommunicatios Satellite
EV	exposure value
EVC	Eurovision Control Centre
EVR	electronic video recording
EXR	extended range
ext.	exterior
EZEF	Evangelisches Zentrum für entwicklungsbezogene Filmarbeit

F

f	focus
FACTS	Federation of Australian Commercial Television Stations
FAKI	Fachnormenausschuß Kinotechnik für Film und Fernsehen
FAT	ferngesteuerter, adressierbarer Teilnehmerkonverter
FAT	Filmabtaster
FAZ	Filmaufzeichnung
FBAS-Signal	Farb-, Bild-, Austast- und Synchronsignal
FBW	Filmbewertungsstelle Wiesbaden
fc	foot candles
FCC	Federal Communication Commision
FDAT	Farb-Dia-Abtaster
FEBC	Far East Broadcasting Company, Manila

FELIX	European filmmaward
FEMI	Flemish European Media Institute, Brüssel
FEP	Föderation Europäischer Photographen
FER	film editor's report
FET	Feldeffekt-Transistor, field effect transistor
FFA	Filmförderungsanstalt
FFG	Filmförderungsgesetz
FFV	Film- und Fernsehverband
FKTG	Fernseh- und Kinotechnische Gesellschaft
FM	Frequenzmodulation
FMSR	Fachnormenausschuß »Messen, Steuern, Regeln für technische Prozesse«
FPS	frames per second
FQ	frequency equalizer
FS	Fernsehen
FS	full shot
FSK	Freiwillige Selbstkontrolle der Filmwirtschaft
FSM	Fernsehstudio München
ft	foot
FTC	Federal Trade Commision
FTC	Fuji Telecasting Company
FTG	Fernsehtechnische Gesellschaft
FTZ	Fernmeldetechnisches Zentralamt
FWU	Institut für Film und Bild in Wissenschaft und Unterricht
FX	effects

G

G	Gauss
G	Giga
GA	Gemeinschaftsantennenanlage
GBC	Ghana Broadcasting Corporation
GDBA	Genossenschaft Deutscher Bühnenangehöriger
GEAR	Group of European Audience Researchers
GEMA	Gesellschaft für musikalische Aufführungs- und mechanische Vervielfältigungsrechte
GEMM	Groupe d'etudes des mass media
GEP	Gemeinschaftswerk der Evangelischen Publizistik

GEZ	Gebühreneinzugszentrale der öffentlich-rechtlichen Rundfunkanstalten
GFF	Gesellschaft für Film- und Fernsehwissenschaft
GfK	Gesellschaft für Konsum-, Markt- und Absatzforschung
GFK	Glasfaserkabel
GfU	Gesellschaft zur Förderung der Unterhaltungselektronik
GGA	Großgemeinschafts-Antennenanlage
GHz	Gigahertz
GPI	Gesellschaft für programmierte Instruktion
gpi	Gesellschaft für Pädagogik und Information
GS	Geprüfte Sicherheit
GSOC	German Space Operation Centre
GÜFA	Gesellschaft zur Übernahme und Wahrnehmung von Fernsehaufführungsrechten
GUV	Gesellschaft zur Verfolgung von Urheberrechtsverletzungen
G/V	general view
GVL	Gesellschaft zur Verwertung von Leistungsschutzrechten

H

HA	Hauptabteilung
HADS	hole accumulated diode sensor
HAM	Hamburgische Anstalt für neue Medien
HBO	Home Box Office
HBST	high-band saticon trinicon camera tube
HC	high current, heavy current
HDEP	high definition electronic production
HDFS	high definition film system
HDRC	High Dynamic Range CMOS
HDTV	high definition television
HET	Health Education Telecommunication
HF	high frequency
HF	Hörfunk
HFF	Hochschule für Fernsehen und Film
HFR	hold for release
HHI	Heinrich-Hertz-Institut für Nachrichtentechnik
HI	high-intensity

HID	high intensity discharger
HiFi	high-fidelity
HI-OVIS	highly interactive optical visual informations system
HK	Hefnerkerze
HK	high key
HKR	Hauptkontrollraum
HK/TVB	Hongkong Television Broadcasts
HMI	hydrargym medium arc-length iodide
HP	home passed
HQ	high quality
HR	Hessischer Rundfunk
HS	high-speed
HSR	Hauptschaltraum
HT	high tension
HTM	high-definition television monitor
HTN	Home Theater Network
HUT	home using television
HVN	Home View Network
Hz	Hertz

I

I	interlaced
IABM	International Association of Broadcasting Manufactures
IAC	Institute of Amateur Cinematographers, GB
IADM	Internationale Assoziation deutschsprachiger Medien
IAK	Internationale Arbeitsgemeinschaft für Kommunikationspädagogik
IAPA	Inter-American Press Association
IARU	The Internationale Amateur Radio Union
IATSE	International Alliance of Theatrical State Employees
IAWRT	International Association of Women in Radio and Television
IBA	Independent Broadcasting Authority, GB
IBA	Israel Broadcasting Authority
IBC	International Broadcasting Convention
IBEW	International Brotherhood of Electrical Workers
IBI	International Broadcasting Institute
IBS	International Broadcasters Society

IBTS	Italian Broadcasting and Telecommunication Show
IBU	International Broadcasting Union
IC	integrated circuit
ICB	International Christian Broadcasters
ICR	Instituto Cubano de Radiodifusión
ICU	International Communications Union
IEE	The Institution of Electrical Engeneers, GB
IEEE	Institute of Electrical and Electronics Engineers
IF	intermediate frequency
IFA	International Federation of Actors
IFA	Internationale Funkausstellung Berlin
IFB	Internationale Filmfestspiele Berlin
IFCIC	Institut pour le financement du cinéma et des industries culturelle
IFFA	International Federation of Film Archives
IFJ	International Federation of Journalists
IFN	Institut für Nachrichtentechnik an der FU Berlin
IFPI	International Federation of Phonogram and Videogram Producers
IFTA	International Film and Television Archives
IFTC	International Film and Television Council
IFV	Internationaler Fernmeldevertrag
IGR	Interessengemeinschaft für Rundfunkschutzrechte
IHF	Institute of High Fidelity
IINA	International Islamic News Agency
IKK	Internationale Kommission zum Studium von Kommunikations-problemen
ILR	Independent Local Radio, GB
IM	intermodulation
in	inch
I.N.A.	Institut National de Audiovisuel
INCH	Independent Channel Handler
INRAK	Kommission für Investitionsplanung und Rationalisierung ARD/ZDF
INS	Information Network System
int.	interior
INTELSAT	International Telecommunications Satellite-Consortium
INTERGU	Internationale Gesellschaft für Urheberrecht
INTV	Association of Independent Television Stations
IOJ	International Organisation of Journalists
IP	interpositive

IP	image plus
IPA	Information Publicitée Allemagne
IPI	International Press Institute
ips	inch per second
IPS	Inter Press Services
IR	Infrarot, infra-red
IRT	Institut für Rundfunktechnik
IRV	Instituto Nacional de Radio y Televisión, Kolumbien
ISBO	The Islamic States Broadcasting Services Organization
ISDN	integrated services digital network
ISO	International Standardizing Organisation
IT	interline transfer
IT	Internationaler Ton
ITA	Independent Television Authority
ITA	International Tape Association
ITCA	Independent Television Contractors Association
ITN	Independent Television News
ITU	International Telecommunication Union
ITV	United Kingdom Independent Broadcasting
ITVA	Internationaler Verband der Video-Anwender
IuK	Information und Kommunikation
IVCA	International Visual Communications Association, GB
IvD	Ingenieur vom Dienst
IVPI	Internationale Vereinigung der Phonografischen Industrie
IVW	Informationsgemeinschaft zur Feststellung der Verbreitung von Werbeträgern

J

JBC	Jamaica Broadcasting Corporation
JCIA	Japan Camera Industry Association
JCII	Japan Camera and Optical Instruments Inspection and testing Institute
JECC	Japan Electronic Computer Center
JESA	Japanese Engineering Standards Association
JFF	Institut für Jugend Film und Fernsehen
JP	The Jiji Press, Japan
JPEA	Japan Photographic Enterprisers Asiciation

JPEG	Joint Photographers Expert Group
JPEIA	Japan Photographic Equipment Industrial Association
JPSE	Japan Photographic Studio Equipment Association
JRT	Jugoslovenska Radiotelevizja, Jugoslawien
JTV	Jordan Radio and Television Corporation
JVC	Victor Company of Japan

K

k	kilo
K	Kelvin
K.	Kopierer
Ka-Mi-Tax	Kamera-Miet-Taxi
KBS	Korean Broadcasting System, Süd-Korea
KBTS	Kuwait Broadcasting and Television Service
KEF	Kommission zur Ermittlung des Finanzbedarfs der Rundfunkanstalten Deutschlands
kg	Kilogramm
kHz	Kilohertz
KJF	Kinder- und Jugendfilmzentrum
KKA	Kabelkommunikationsanlage
KKG	Kamerakontrollgerät
KMFB	Gewerkschaft Kunst, Medien, freie Berufe
KMP	Kabel Media Programmgesellschaft
KNA	Katholische Nachrichten Agentur
KNK	Kommission Neue Kommunikationstechniken
KRD	Katholische Rundfunkarbeit
KRO	Katholieke Radio Omroep, Niederlande
KT	Kabeltext
KTA	Kabeltelevisie Amsterdam
KtK	Kommission für den Ausbau des technischen Kommunikationssystems
KTV	Kabel-Television
KWIS	Kommunikationswissenschaftliche Informationsstelle der Pädagogischen Hochschule Freiburg

L

LAD	laboratory aim density
LAR	Landesanstalt für Rundfunkwesen im Saarland
LASER	light amplification by stimulated emission of radiation
LBC	Liberian Broadcasting Corporation
LBJ	Libyan Broadcasting Jamaherya
LCCC	leadless ceramic chip carrier
LCD	liquid crystal display
LC-Filter	low-contrast filter
LCP	local control panel
LED	Licht emittierende Diode, light-emitting diode
LF	low frequency
LfR	Landesanstalt für Rundfunk
LH	low noise – high output
LJB	Libyan Jamahiriya Broadcasting
lm	Lumen
LO	local origination channel
LOP	least objectionable program
LP	long playing
LPR	Landeszentrale für private Rundfunkveranstalter
LPTV	low power television
LR	Linksrheinischer Rundfunky
LR-Signal	Links-Rechts-Signal
LRW	Local Radio Workshop
LS	long shot
LSI	large scale intergration
LT	low tension
LTC	longitudinal time-code
LTS	Libyan Television Service
LUX-SAT	Satellitenprojekt Luxemburg
LV	Laservision
LV	low voltage
LvD	Leiter vom Dienst
LVR	longitudinal video recording
LW	Langwelle
LWL	Lichtwellenleiter

M

M&Smic	middle and side microphones
MA	Media Analyse
MAC	multiplexed analogue components
M and D	master and dups
M and E	music and sound effects
MAP	Media Access Project
M.A.R.C.	MII automated recording/playback cassette system
MASER	micro-wave amplification by stimulated emission of radiation
MATV	master antenna television system
MAZ	Magnetbildaufzeichnung
MBA	Malta Broadcasting Authority
MC	master of ceremonies
MCB	miniature circuit breaker
MCPS	Mechanical Copyright Protection Society, GB
MCR	mobile control room
MCS	medium close shot
MCTV	Manhattan Cable Television
MCU	medium close-up shot
MD	mini-disk
MDZ	Mediendidaktisches Zentrum
MEDIA	Mésure pour encourager le développement de l'industrie de production audiovisuel, Belgien
MENA	Middle East News Agency
MF	medium frequency
MF	median frequency, medium frequency
MGM	Metro-Goldwyn-Meyer
MHz	Megahertz
MIDI	musical instrument digital interface
MIRAG	Mitteldeutsche Rundfunk AG
Mired	micro reciprocal degree
MIT	Massachusetts Institute of Technology, USA
MK	Megakelvin
MKS	MAZ-Kreuzschiene
MLS	medium long shot
MNA	Multi-Network Area
MOD	minimum operating distance

MoMi	Museum of the Moving Image
MOS	Mit-out-Sprache
MPA	Master Photographers Association
MPAA	Motion Picture Association of America
MPEAA	Motion Picture Export Association of America
MPPC	Motion Picture Patents Company
MS	medium shot
MSC	Madison Square Garden Network
MSI	medium scale integration
MTB	Medien und Technik im Bildungsbereich
MTBF	meantime between failures
MTF	modulation transfer function
MTTF	meantime to failures
MTTR	meantime to repair
MTV	Music Television
MTV	Malta Television Service
MÜF	Modulationsübertragungsfunktion
MUSE	multiple sub-nyquist sampling encoding
MW	Megawatt
MW	Mittelwelle

N

NAB	National Association of Broadcasters
NABET	National Association of Broadcast and Employees Technicians
NABTS	North American National Broad Teletext Standard
NAEB	National Association of Educational Broadcasters
NANBA	North American National Broadcaster's Association
NAPM	National Assiciation of Photographic Manufactures
NASA	National Aeronautics and Space Administration
NATKE	National Association of Theatrical and Kine Employees
NATP	National Association of Television Program Executives
NBC	National Broadcasting Company
NCNA	New China News Agency
NCTA	National Cable Television Association
nd	non-descript
ND	neutral density
NDR	Norddeutscher Rundfunk

NET	National Education Television
NET	Nippon Educational Television Company
NF	Niederfrequenz
Ng	no good
NHK	Nippon Hoso Kyokai
NiBC	Nigerian Broadcasting Corporation
NK	Neue Kerze
NK.	Nichtkopierer
növL	nicht öffentlich-beweglicher Landfunk
NOS	Nederlandse Omroepprogramma Stichting
NPACT	National Public Affairs Center for Television
NPR	National Public Radio
NRK	Norsk Rikskringkasting, Norwegen
ns	Nanosekunde
NT	Nationaler Ton
NTI	Nielsen Television Index rating
NTPM	network termination for primary multiplexing access
NTSC	National Television System Comittee
NTT	Nippon Telephone and Telegraph Company, Japan
NTV	Nippon Television Network Corporation, Japan
NÜ	Nachrichtenübertragung

O

OANA	Organization of Asian News Agencies
OB	outside broadcasting
öbL	öffentlicher-beweglicher Landfunk
oc	off-camera
OCP	operation control panel
OCTV	open-circuit television
ODGRT	Oman Directorate General of Radio and Television
OEL	Orts-Empfangsleitung
OEM	original equipment manufacturer
ÖGK	Österreichische Gesellschaft für Kommunikationsfragen
OIRT	Organisation Internationale de Radiodiffusion et Télévision
OK	offener Kanal
ONS	Overseas News Agency, GB
OOF	out of frame

OOP	out-of-pocket expenses
OOV	out of vision
OPD	Oberpostdirektion
OPT	operation prime time
ORACLE	optional reception of announcement by coded line electronics
ORB	Ostdeutscher Rundfunk Brandenburg, D
ORF	Österreichischer Rundfunk
ORTF	Office de Radiodiffusion-Télévision Française
ORTN	Office de Radiodiffusion-Télévision du Niger
ORTS	Office de Radiodiffusion-Télévision du Sénégal
OS	off screen
OSD	on screen display
OSL	Orts-Sendeleitung
OSS	over-the-shoulder shot
OTA	Office of Technology Assessment
OTI	Organización de la Televisión Iberoamericana
OTO	one time only
O-Ton	Originalton
OTP	Office of Telecommunications Policy
OTS	Orbital Test Satellite

P

p	progressive Bildaufzeichnung
p	piko
p	pond
pA	Pikoampère
PA	production assistant
PA	public-address system
PA	The Press Association
PAL	phase alternation line
PAL	programmable array logic
PAR	parabolic aluminized reflector
PAS	Produktionsaußenstelle
PAT	Panamericana Televisión
PBS	Public Broadcasting System
PC	personal computer
PCM	puls-code-modulation

PC spot	plano-convex spotlight
PD	public domain
PDA	pulse distribution amplifier
PDA	post deflection acceleration
PE	Polyester
PFA	Press Foundation of Asia
PFL	pre-fade listen
PG	parental guidance suggested
Pixel	picture element
PKK	Projektgesellschaft für Kabel- und Kommunikation
PL	party line
PL	Produktionsleiter
PLL	phase locked loop
PLUGE	picture line-up generating equipment
PM	Phasen-Modulation
PMA	Photo Marketing Association
PMA	Photo Marketing Association Convention and Trade Show
PMDA	Photo Manufactures and Distributors Association
PMT	photo mechanical transfer
POC	production office coordinator
PoI	point-of-interest
PoS	point-of-sale
POV	point-of-view shot
PP	power pack
pp	peak-to-peak
PPM	peak programme meter
PPM	pulse position modulation
pps	pictures per second
PPT	Projected Picture Trust, GB
PPV	pay-per-view
PRF	pulse repetition frequency
PRI	Radio Republik Indonesia
PRS	Performing Rights Society, GB
PSA	public-service announcement
psF	progressiv segmentiertes Frame
PSSC	Public Service Satellite Consortium
PTC	Pakistan Television Corporation
PTV	Public Television, USA

PU	pick-up
PWM	pulse-width modulation
PZM	pressure-zone-microphone

Q

QA	quality insurance
Q-I.	quartz iodide lamp
QIL	quad-in-line
QPSK	quadrature phase-shift keying
QTBS	Quatar Television and Broadcasting Service

R

R	restricted
RADAR	radio detecting and ranging
RAI	Radiotelevisione Italiana
RB	Ritzaus Bureau
RBC	Rhodesia Broadcasting Corporation
RBI	Radio Berlin International, DDR
RBT	Rundfunkbetriebstechnik
RCA	Radio Corporation of America
RCT	Radio Caracas Television
RCU	remote control unit
RDD	random digital dialing
RDP	Radiodifusao Portugesa
RDS	Radio-Daten-System
REM	Radio Emisora de Madrid
RESI	Rechnerunterstütztes elektronisches System zur Informationsverteilung
REVAS	Rechnerunterstützte Vorbereitung und Abwicklung von Sendungen
RF	radio frequency
Rf.	Rundfunk
RFC	Radio Forces Canadienne
RFE	Radio Free Europe
RFFU	Rundfunk-Fernseh-Film-Union
RGB	rot-grün-blau

RI	Radio Iran
RIAA	Recording Industries Association of America
RIAS	Radio im amerikanischen Sektor
RITE	Research Institute of Telecommunication and Economics
RKO	Radio-Keith-Orpheum
RL	Radiodiffusion Libanaise
RL	Radio Liberty, USA
RMC	Radio Monte Carlo
R.M.S.	root mean square
RNE	Radio Nacional de España
RNS	Radiodiffusion Nationale du Sénégale
ROS	run of schedule
RPS	Royal Photographic Society, GB
RPT	Radio de la Plata, Argentinien
RP unit	rear-projection unit
RT	Radio Tanzania
RTA	Radiodiffusion Algérienne
RTB	Radiodiffusion-Télévision Belge
RTBF	Radio-Télévision Belge de la Communauté française
RTE	Radio Telefis Eireann, Irland
RTG	Radiodiffusion Télévision Gabonaise, Gabun
RTI	Radiodiffusion Télévision Ivoirienne
RTL	Radio Tele Luxemburg
RTM	Radiodiffusion-Télévision Marocaine
RTNDA	Radio/Television News Director's Association
RTP	Radio Televisão Portuguesa
RTR	Reuters
RTS	Royal Television Society, GB
RTT	Radiodiffusion-Télévision Tunisienne
RTV	Rediffusion Television, Hongkong
RTZ	return to zero
RU	remote unit
RUDI	Rundfunk-, Dokumentations- und Informationssystem
RuF	Rundfunk und Fernsehen
RUV	Rikisútvarpith-Sjónvarp, Island
RV	Radio Vaticana
RZ	Rechenzentrum

S

SABC	South African Broadcasting Corporation
SAG	Screen Actors Guild
SAP	Sendeablaufplan
SAST	Sendeablaufsteuerung
SAW	Sendeabwicklung
SAWA	Screen Advertising World Association
sb	Stilb
SBCA	Satellite Broadcasting and Communications Association, USA
SBS	Satellite Business System
SCA	Subsidiary Communications Authorisation, USA
SCG	Screen Cartoonists Guild
sci-fi	science-fiction
SCRIPT	Support for Creative Independent Talent
SCU	sync coupler unit
SCU	shutter control unit
sd	sound dub
SDA	Schweizerische Depeschen Agentur
SDK	Stiftung Deutsche Kinemathek Berlin
SDR	Süddeutscher Rundfunk
SDRW	SDR Werbung
SE	sound-effects
Secam	sequentielle à memoire
SEG	Screen Extras Guild
SEG	special effect generator
SEPMAG	separate magnetic sound
SES	Société Européenne des Satellites
SFB	Sender Freies Berlin
SFBW	SFB Werbung
SFD	Society of Film Distributors, GB
S/F/K-Verband	Szenenbildner-Filmarchitekten-Kostumbildner-Verband
SFP	Société Française de Production et de Création AV
SFRV	Schweizerische Fernseh- und Radio-Vereinigung
SFT	Société Française de Télécommunications
SFX	sound effects
SGKM	Schweizerische Gesellschaft für Kommunikations- und Medienwissenschaft

SHF	super high frequency
SHO	Showtime, USA
sia	storage instantaneous audiometer
SIAD	Society of Industrial Artists and Designers, GB
SIN	Spanish International Network
SINAD	signal to noise and distortion
SIS	sound-in-sync
SIT	silicon-intensified target
SK	Sendekomplex
SKS	Sendekreuzschiene
SL	Sendeleitung
SLR	single-lens-reflex
SMATV	Satellite Master-Antenna Television
SMC	slow-motion controler
SMPTE	Society of Motion Picture and Television Engineers
SMS	Multiservice Satellite System
S/N	signal noise ratio
SNC	Satellite News Channel
SNG	satellite news gathering
SNV	satellite news vehicle
SOF	sound-on-film
SOFIRAD	Société Financière de Radiodiffusion
SORADOM	Société de Radiodiffusion de la France D'outre-Mer
SP	standard play
SP	superior perfomance
Sp-FX	special effects
SPG	sync-pulse generator
SPIDEM	Spitzenverband Deutsche Musik
SPIO	Spitzenorganisation der Filmwirtschaft
SPL	sound pressure level
SPN	Satellite Program Network
SPSE	The Society for Imaging Science and Technology
SQ	Stereo-Quadrophonie
SR	spectral recording
SR	Saarländischer Rundfunk
SR	Sveriges Radio, Schweden
SRC	Société Radio Canada
SRF	Radio- und Fernsehgesellschaft der deutschen und rätoromanischen Schweiz

SRG	Schweizerische Radio- und Fernsehgesellschaft
SRT	Schule für Rundfunktechnik
SSI	small scale integration
SSR	Société Suisse de Radiodiffusion et Télévision
SSS	Southern Satellite System
SSTV	slow-scanning television
SSVR	solid state video recorder
STC	Satellite Television Corporation
STC	single time-code
STS	Sudan Television Service
STV	subscription television
SUISA	Schweizerische Verwertungsgesellschaft
S-VHS	Super-VHS
SVR	super video recording
SVT	Sveriges Television, Schweden
SW	short waves
SWF	Südwestfunk
SWG	standard wire gauge
sync.	synchronisation

T

t	Tonne
T	transmission
TAF	telecine analysis film
TAM	Television Audience Measurment
T and A	tits and asses
TASS	Telegrafnoje Agentsto Sovetskovo Sajusa
TB	Tonbandgerät
TBA	Television Bureau of Advertising
TBA	to be announced
TBC	time base corrector
TBD	to be determined
TBS	Tokyo Broadcasting System
TC	time-code
TCM	Tele-Cadena Mexicana
TD	technical director
TDF	Télédiffusion de France

TELCOM	Telefunken-Compandersystem
TF	till forbid
TL	Radiodiffusion Libanaise / Tele-Liban
Tobis	Tonbildsyndikat
TOPICS	total on-line programm information system
TransTel	Gesellschaft für Deutsche Fernseh-Transkription
TRT	Türkiye Radyo-Televizyon Kurumu
TSA	total survey area
TSS	Televidenie Sowjetskowo Sojusa
TSW	Television South West Holding
TTL	through-the-lens
TV	television
TVA	Télé-Diffuseurs Associés, Kanada
TVC	TV Chile
TVE	Radiotelevision Espanola
TVHH	television households
TVP	Polske Radio i Telewizja
TVQ	television quotient
TVR	Radiodifuziunea si Teledifuziunea Ramania
TWR	Trans World Radio, Monaco
TX	Transmitter

U

UACC	USA-Columbia Cable Television
UAERTV	United Arab Emirates Radio and Television
UCCTV	Corporación de Television de la Universidad Católica, Chile
UCLAP	Unión Catolica Lation-Americana de la Press
UDK	Union Deutscher Künstleragenten
Üp	Übergabepunkt
UER	Union Européene de Radiodiffusion
UFITA	Archiv für Urheber-, Film-, Funk- und Theaterrecht
UHF	ultra high frequency
UIPRE	Union Internationale de la Presse Radiotechnique et Electrique
UIT	Union Internationale de Télécommunications
UKW	Ultrakurzwelle
ULCRA	Union Latinoamericana y del Caribe de Radiodiffusion
ULR	Unabhängige Landesanstalt für das Rundfunkwesen Schleswig-

	Holstein
U-Musik	Unterhaltungsmusik
UNDA	Catholic Broadcasting Organization
UNTV	United Nations Television
UPI	United Press International
UPU	Universal Postal Union
UrhG	Urhebergesetz
UrhG	Urhebergesetz, D
URSI	Union Radio-Scientifique Internationale
URTI	Université Radiophonique Télévisuelle Internationale
URTNA	Union des Radiodiffusions et Télévisuelle Nationales d'Afrique
USP	United States Network Pool
USSB	United States Satellite Broadcasting
USTV	United Satellite Television
UTC	Universal Time co-ordinated
UV	Ultra-violett
UVR	Unfallverhütungsrichtlinien ARD/ZDF
Ü-Wagen	Übertragungswagen

V

V	Volt
VCA	voltage controlled amplifier
VCC	video compact cassette
VCR	video cassette recorder
VCU	very close-up shot
vdav	Verband Deutscher Amateurfotografen-Vereine
VDF	Verband der Filmverleiher
VDFE	Verband Deutscher Filmexporteure
VDT	Verband Deutscher Tonmeister
VF	view finder
VF	Videofrequent
VFF	Verwertungsgesellschaft der Film- und Fernsehproduzenten
VGB	Verwertungsgesellschaft Bild
VGP	Vereinigung von Grossisten für den Photohandel
VG Wort	Verwertungsgesellschaft Wort
VHF	very high frequency
VHS	video home system

VHS-HQ	VHS high-quality
VI	volume indicator
VIP	Vereinigung der Industriefilmproduzenten
VISS	video index search system
VITC	vertical interval time-code
VLF	very low frequency
VLP	video long play
VO	voice over
VoA	Voice of America
VPS	viewers per set
VPS	video program system
VRC	video recording camera
VRFF	Vereinigung der Rundfunk-, Film- und Fernsehschaffenden
Vs	Voltsekunde
VSU	variable speed unit
VTFF	Verband technischer Betriebe für Film und Fernsehen
VTR	videotape recorder
VU meter	volume units meter

W

W/A	wide angle
WACC	World Association for Christian Communication
WARC	World Administrative Radio Conference
WCC	Warners Cable Communications
WCI	Warners Communications Inc.
WDR	Westdeutscher Rundfunk
WFS	Werbefernsehen Saar
WGA	Writers Guild of America
Whl.	Wiederholung
WIK	Wissenschaftliches Institut für Kommunikationsdienste der Deutschen Bundespost
WIS	Werbung im Südwestfunk
WST	World System Teletext
WTA	World Teleport Association
WTN	World Television News
WWF	Westdeutsches Werbefernsehen
WWUYS	World Wide Unified Videotex Standard

X

X	frame
X-copy	transferred sound master
XFER/XFR	transfer
XLS	extra long shot

Y

YLE	Oy Yleisradio, Finnland

Z

ZAW	Zentralausschuß der Werbewirtschaft
ZB	zoom back
ZD	Zentraldisposition
ZDF	Zweites Deutsches Fernsehen
ZF	Zwischenfrequenz
ZFP	Zentrale Fortbildung Programm-Mitarbeiter ARD/ ZDF
ZI	zoom in
ZKS	Zentralkreuzschiene
ZKTV	Zweiweg-Kabelfernsehen
ZO	zoom out
ZSL	Zentrale Sendeleitung
ZVEH	Zentralverband der Deutschen Elektrohandwerke
ZVEI	Zentralverband Elektrotechnik- und Elektronikindustrie